KEYWORDS IN DESIGN THINKING

A LEXICAL PRIMER FOR TECHNICAL COMMUNICATORS & DESIGNERS

Foundations and Innovations in Technical and Professional Communication

Series Editor: Lisa Melonçon

Series Associate Editors: Kristin Marie Bivens and Sherena Huntsman

The Foundations and Innovations in Technical and Professional Communication series publishes work that is necessary as a base for the field of technical and professional communication (TPC), addresses areas of central importance within the field, and engages with innovative ideas and approaches to TPC. The series focuses on presenting the intersection of theory and application/practice within TPC and is intended to include both monographs and co-authored works, edited collections, digitally enhanced work, and innovative works that may not fit traditional formats (such as works that are longer than a journal article but shorter than a book).

The WAC Clearinghouse and University Press of Colorado are collaborating so that these books will be widely available through free digital distribution and low-cost print editions. The publishers and the series editors are committed to the principle that knowledge should freely circulate and have embraced the use of technology to support open access to scholarly work.

Other Books in the Series

Kate Crane and Kelli Cargile Cook (Eds.), *User Experience as Innovative Academic Practice* (2022)
Joanna Schreiber and Lisa Melonçon (Eds.), *Assembling Critical Components: A Framework for Sustaining Technical and Professional Communication* (2022)
Michael J. Klein (Ed.), *Effective Teaching of Technical Communication: Theory, Practice, and Application* (2021).

KEYWORDS IN DESIGN THINKING

A LEXICAL PRIMER FOR TECHNICAL COMMUNICATORS & DESIGNERS

Edited by Jason C. K. Tham

The WAC Clearinghouse
wac.colostate.edu
Fort Collins, Colorado

University Press of Colorado
upcolorado.com
Denver, Colorado

The WAC Clearinghouse, Fort Collins, Colorado 80523

University Press of Colorado, Denver, Colorado 80202

ISBN 978-1-64215-172-5 (PDF) | 978-1-64215-173-2 (ePub) | 978-1-64642-394-1 (pbk.)

DOI 10.37514/TPC-B.2022.1725

Produced in the United States of America

Library of Congress Cataloging-in-Publication Data

Names: Tham, Jason Chew Kit, 1990– editor.
Title: Keywords in design thinking : a lexical primer for technical communicators & designers / edited by Jason C.K. Tham.
Description: Fort Collins, Colorado : The WAC Clearinghouse ; Boulder, Colorado : University Press of Colorado, [2022] | Series: Foundations and innovations in technical and professional communication | Includes bibliographical references.
Identifiers: LCCN 2022059676 (print) | LCCN 2022059677 (ebook) | ISBN 9781646423941 (paperback) | ISBN 9781642151725 (adobe pdf) | ISBN 9781642151732 (epub)
Subjects: LCSH: Problem solving. | Creative thinking. | Communication of technical information.
Classification: LCC BF449 .K47 2022 (print) | LCC BF449 (ebook) | DDC 153.4/3—dc23/eng/20230222
LC record available at https://lccn.loc.gov/2022059676
LC ebook record available at https://lccn.loc.gov/2022059677

Copyeditor: Meg Vezzu
Designer: Mike Palmquist
Series Editor: Lisa Melonçon
Series Associate Editors: Kristin Marie Bivens and Sherena Huntsman

The WAC Clearinghouse supports teachers of writing across the disciplines. Hosted by Colorado State University, it brings together scholarly journals and book series as well as resources for teachers who use writing in their courses. This book is available in digital formats for free download at wac.colostate.edu.

Founded in 1965, the University Press of Colorado is a nonprofit cooperative publishing enterprise supported, in part, by Adams State University, Colorado State University, Fort Lewis College, Metropolitan State University of Denver, University of Alaska Fairbanks, University of Colorado, University of Denver, University of Northern Colorado, University of Wyoming, Utah State University, and Western Colorado University. For more information, visit upcolorado.com.

Land Acknowledgment. The Colorado State University Land Acknowledgment can be found at https://landacknowledgment.colostate.edu.

■ Contents

■ Acknowledgments

A project like this takes a village to complete. First and foremost, I am thankful—like, *big-time* thankful—for the patience and trust the contributors of this collection have given to me and this book. Without them this volume wouldn't exist. COVID was hard. The lingering effects are even harder. Doing anything remotely "productive" is challenging no matter where we are right now. I thank the contributors for their generosity and flexibility. They were courteous and pleasant even when everything else was just dreadful. They made it relatively fun to edit a book.

I was inspired by Guy McHenry, who had collaborated with his students to produce an open-access keywords collection on surveillance studies (https://pressbooks.pub/surveillancestudies) in 2019. Then a freshly minted Ph.D. graduate, I thought to myself that similar efforts could be made for the topic of "design thinking"—an area of interest I developed while dissertating, thanks in part to the introduction by my mentors Ann Hill Duin and Joe Moses. Patrick Bruch, with whom I have taken classes in writing studies, has taught me that one way to learn about any given subject matter is to ask the question, "What is . . ." Hence the underlining question for this project: *What is design thinking?* Attempting to answer that question, I was brought back into reality by the teachings of Lee-Ann Kastman Breuch, who reminded me the importance of *explaining things . . .* as it's the bread-and-butter of a technical communicator's job. What background does one need to know? How might they apply a certain concept or skill? What are the pedagogical implications? Thus the motivation of this project. With these early experiences and unearned confidence, I went ahead and drafted a call for contributions for this project in the summer of 2019 and sent it into the listserv ether. It was a speculative move, to say the least. Yet, to my surprise, many people seemed to be fond of this idea. My inbox was soon filled with questions and queries about the project, and I found myself feeling accountable for the scholars and practitioners who saw it as an opportunity to *explain* what it is that they do with design thinking, whether in the classroom, at work, or with their communities.

And *explain* they did. This volume is the evidence.

To explain is also to inform and to educate. Sometimes, it takes more than just words and theories. Evidently, good explanations are paired with practical applications and recommendations. Thanks to the helpful feedback from the editors and reviewers of the Foundations and Innovations in Technical and Professional Communication series, *Keywords* authors were able to contextualize and situate their explanations within disciplinary settings. After rounds of revision and conversations, I am happy to see *Keywords* take its current form. I thank Lisa Melonçon and her team for making this book a reality.

Finally, I would be remiss to close without a shout-out to my family: my partner, Kamm, who patiently listened to all the ideas I had for this project (thank you for all the love and support, especially during times when I was about to give up), and to the furry babies—Cornelius, Malia, and Athena—for their unconditional affection whether or not this book was going to make it; they just want the pettings.

KEYWORDS IN DESIGN THINKING

A LEXICAL PRIMER FOR TECHNICAL COMMUNICATORS & DESIGNERS

Introduction to Design Thinking & *Keywords*

Jason Tham
TEXAS TECH UNIVERSITY

Luke Thominet
FLORIDA INTERNATIONAL UNIVERSITY

■ What is Design Thinking?

We open this text by explaining **design thinking** in what we hope to be a simple and direct language. Our goal is to use this initial description as a reference point that we can return to throughout our discussion in this book, even as we begin to complicate the idea of design thinking later.

So, what is design thinking, exactly?

In short, design thinking is an approach for creating solutions to difficult problems. It is simultaneously a way of thinking about problems (i.e., a creative mindset) as well as a process for seeking resolutions to those problems (i.e., a problem-solving methodology). People typically use design thinking in response to complex problems that have no easy or definite solution, namely "wicked problems" (see Rittel & Webber, 1973). Design thinking projects are also fundamentally human-centered: They focus on understanding and addressing people's real concerns. Finally, the design thinking process encourages collaboration, creativity, and responsiveness. It asks diverse teams of designers to create a broad set of potential solutions and then to test those solutions with real stakeholders.

If this definition sounds ambiguous, it is because ambiguity *is* the nature of design thinking. As we note below, a benefit of the design thinking mindset is that it asks practitioners to consider the situation, problem, and audience, without assumptions about solutions. This nonlinear approach can benefit projects that do not have straightforward ways of finding or applying solutions. It is this openness to ambiguity and exploration that makes design thinking stand out in design frameworks, including many of those used in technical and professional communication (TPC) projects today. Design thinking is a unique exploratory *lens* for problem-solving that offers a flexible, heuristic approach to innovation.

■ A Sample Application of Design Thinking

As you will learn in this book, design thinking is a concept claimed both by academics and by industry, often with somewhat incompatible goals and incentives. We will explore the variance between definitions of design thinking in

DOI: https://doi.org/10.37514/TPC-B.2022.1725.1.3

greater detail below, but first, we want to ground this introduction further with a brief example.

Design thinking has been implemented in a wide range of social and technological innovation projects. For example, Jeanne Liedtka, Andrew King, and Kevin Bennett (2013) described ten design thinking projects, including projects that focused on creating better trade shows, improving business-to-business marketing, making customer support experiences more enjoyable, and developing a system for subsidizing meals for the elderly. For a more specific example, we can look at how the Golden Gate Regional Center (GGRC), which provides support for people with developmental disabilities, used design thinking to revise their process for assessing and onboarding clients (Sutton & Hoyt, 2016).

At the outset of the project, the GGRC investigated the experiences of clients and then mapped their own work processes in relation to clients' experiences. This mapping activity helped them identify a number of different "pain points" for clients, including the extended duration of the onboarding process and the need to repeatedly travel to the GGRC for required appointments. In response, the design thinking team collaboratively imagined several ways to address these problems. One of their more innovative ideas was to use a Winnebago motorhome as a mobile office so the entire GGRC team could travel directly to the clients' neighborhoods and complete all of the appointments at one time. They then prototyped this idea by renting a Winnebago and testing the method for one day. While this strategy processed assessments "10 weeks faster than normal," it was also too expensive to sustain and scale up (Sutton & Hoyt, 2016). So, the design thinking team took what they learned from the experience and developed new prototypes, such as GGRC open houses in local neighborhoods and mobile social workers who used tablets to serve families in their own homes.

The above example is often what design thinking processes look like. An organization or community faces a significant and intractable problem. Rather than patching small issues or relying on well-established solutions, the organization seeks to understand users' experiences and uses this knowledge to reframe the problem. Then, they collaboratively seek innovative solutions, no matter how far-fetched those solutions might initially seem. Finally, they directly prototype and test potential solutions with real users to gauge their effectiveness. There are, of course, reasonable criticisms of this process. As we can see in the example, design thinking requires a significant investment of time and resources. It can also lead to detours, such as the Winnebago prototype, which are not feasible at scale. And it is sometimes difficult to determine a stopping point in design thinking projects, or a moment when prototyping and testing end, and a selected solution is fully implemented. In sum, design thinking is not fit for every context and problem. But in the right context, design thinking can help organizations to see complex problems anew while seeking imaginative solutions that might fall outside the scope of other design frameworks. With this basic understanding of design thinking, let's take a look at how it came about.

■ A Brief History of Design Thinking

The historical development of design thinking is generally agreed upon. Since it has been written about in length already (Cross, 2001, 2007; Kimbell, 2011), we will only cover the key figures in its development here as pertaining to TPC interests. Most often, design thinking is traced back to mid-twentieth century efforts to systemize all forms of design as a singular science. In the early 1960s, Buckminster Fuller (2019) began calling for a "design science revolution" in order to meet the emerging global human and environmental needs (p. 31). Then, in *The Sciences of the Artificial*, originally published in 1969, Herbert Simon (1996) argued that framing design as a science would create "a body of intellectually tough, analytic, partly formalizable, partly empirical, teachable doctrine about the design process" (p. 112). He also simultaneously expanded the purview of design to encompass a wide range of work: "Everyone designs who devises courses of action aimed at changing existing situations into preferred ones" (Simon, 1996, p. 111).

Then, in the 1970s, these arguments for a universal design science began to be questioned. Among the most important developments of this time was Horst Rittel and Melvin Webber's (1973) coining of the term *wicked problems* to refer to problems that are ill-defined and that have no definitive solution. Notably, they argued that wicked problems could not be solved in a scientific manner (Rittel & Webber, 1973, p. 160). Richard Buchanan (1992) later argued that designers mainly dealt with just these sorts of wicked problems.

The 1980s continued this movement away from the rationalized approach of design science and toward theories of design that emphasized user participation and satisfactory resolutions to problems. First, Nigel Cross (1982) sought to establish design as a coherent discipline by positioning it against the sciences and the humanities. Then, Donald Schön (1983) introduced the idea of design as reflection-in-action, which connects doing and thinking as complementary activities (p. 280). Schön also argued that design theory had traditionally ignored problem-setting, which sought to establish the parameters of a problem rather than taking them as givens. Finally, the term *design thinking* was formally coined in Peter Rowe's (1987) book with a title of the same name. In this book, he analyzed the practices of architects and developed a heuristic analysis of how they approached the design process. Notably, his text also emphasized the iterative nature of design while also outlining a process of analysis and evaluation similar to later models.

During this same period, the rise of personal computers and mobile technologies in the West led to a surge in attention to user experience (UX) and human-centered design (HCD). Designers and UX professionals created ways for researching users' behavior and reactions to these unprecedented products, and invented models for ensuring human-centered technology. For an effective account of these models and human factor research methods, we recommend Robert Johnson's (1998) *User-Centered Technology*. Design thinking as a lens for understanding problems and advocating for users benefited from the UX and

HCD perspectives. While not necessarily interchangeable in terms of the guiding principles among these approaches, design thinking, UX, and HCD share common goals. When applied to TPC, all of them aim to affect positive innovation. Each of the approaches, however, contains its own ideologies and emphases in value. Well-known scholar-practitioners like JoAnn Hackos, Ginny Redish, and Patricia Sullivan have made observations about the emergent characteristics in these approaches during this time:

- Writing is design; TPC can apply a user-centered mindset to create usable texts; design-centric methods may afford new understanding of the relationships between designers, systems, and users (Hackos, 1984, 1997)
- HCD protocols like user and task analyses would enhance TPC work; situational analysis can contribute to better usability design (Hackos & Redish, 1998)
- Usability studies should expand to focus on human experience (Sullivan, 1989)

This brief list of TPC scholarship demonstrates the field's attention to design methods via UX and HCD practices. Although the term *design thinking* had not appeared in TPC scholarship then, its essential traits were traceable in these early UX and HCD discussions. Design thinking adds to these discussions the potential benefits of "empathy" as an ideology for user research and the reliance of "radical collaboration" to achieve more desirable design outcomes. This new mindset has slowly influenced UX and HCD work today, in return.

The 1990s and early 2000s saw the establishment of the most common formulations of design thinking. The design consulting firm IDEO—which worked on Apple's first computer mouse—was founded in 1991 and quickly popularized its version of the design thinking process. Several other companies subsequently customized and publicized their own design thinking processes, including IBM Enterprise Design and the British Design Council. Probably the best known advocate for design thinking education, the Hasso Plattner Institute of Design at Stanford (more commonly known as the d.school), was founded in 2005 by key members of IDEO. IDEO employees and d.school faculty were simultaneously publishing numerous popular press books to further publicize design thinking approaches in both business and life, including Tom Kelley and Jonathan Littman's (2001) *The Art of Innovation*, Tim Brown's (2009) *Change by Design*, and Tina Seelig's (2015) *Insight Out: Get Ideas Out of Your Head and into the World*. The next section will describe the design thinking process as popularized in these texts in more detail.

■ The Design Thinking Process

The various design consultants and schools, as described above, each have their own model of the design thinking process. IDEO (2015) currently describes it as three recursive activities of inspiration, ideation, and implementation. IBM (2018) describes it as a "continuous loop of observing, reflecting, and making" (p. 4). And the British Design Council (2019) depicts it as a "double diamond" across four stages: discover, define, develop, and deliver. But the widely known model is the d.school's five phases of the design thinking process: empathize, define, ideate, prototype, test (see Figure 1). In general, these design thinking phases are nonlinear and recursive, so they can respond to the specific contexts of the local problem space (d.school, 2010, p. 5). The goal of the empathize phase is to understand the experiences and perspectives of people in the context of the design challenge. Designers typically interview stakeholders, observe analogous activities, and develop ***empathy***[1] maps. Designers then use this research during the definition phase to support accurate problem-setting. As Schön (1983) noted, real-world problems do not come to designers clearly defined; instead, designers construct a problem definition from uncertain and sometimes contradictory information. The ideation phase seeks to create a range of potential solutions to the design problem. Ideation often has the goal of divergent thinking, or the practice of going wide to develop creative and innovative solutions. Ideation typically involves multidisciplinary teams creating ideas through active and visual design exercises, such as affinity clustering and journey mapping. Then, during the rapid prototyping phase, designers create visual and/or material representations of several potential solutions that they can test with real users. The testing phase is then used to collect feedback on potential solutions in order to support iteration on existing prototypes.

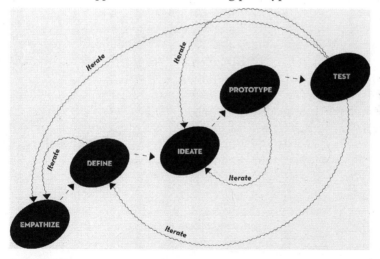

Figure 1. The five iterative components of design thinking: empathize, define, ideate, prototype, and test. Image created by Tham, adapted from the Interaction Design Foundation's model (n.d.), an online educational resource for user experience (UX) researchers and designers.

---

1. Bold italicized keywords in this introduction are terms included in this book. Refer to the table of contents for page numbers.

For technical communicators, this framework provides a guided yet flexible means to good design. But it is not a prescribed workflow. Rather, the framework seeks to illustrate the mindsets of design thinking and to orient technical communicators to the work of design and problem-solving. More importantly, design thinking mirrors and promotes the values that TPC, as a field, advocates for—as seen in our constant attention to user-centeredness, accessibility, creativity, ethical design, evidence-based solutions, participatory methods, etc. We'll explore these intersections between design thinking and technical communication in more depth later, but now we'll look at criticisms of design thinking.

■ Critiques of Design Thinking

As the formalized design thinking process has become widely used over the past two decades, many people have begun to question its efficacy. For example, Lisa Melonçon stated in an interview, "I've never seen design thinking work. . . . it looks great as a theoretical model, but I just haven't been able to ever see it actually work to its fullest potential" (qtd. in Pope-Ruark, 2019). Melonçon's primary argument here was that the formalized design thinking process was time-consuming and resource-intensive and that most projects used shortcuts which undermined the intended results of the process. Some industry practitioners have echoed this perception, calling design thinking a "failed experiment" (Nussbaum, 2011) or even saying that it "is a boondoggle" and "delusional" (Vinsel, 2018). In response to these criticisms, there have been numerous attempts to make the design thinking process more responsive and effective. For example, Kees Dorst (2011) sought to improve design thinking by focusing explicitly on abductive reasoning (or drawing probable conclusions from incomplete observations) and problem framing. And Lucy Kimbell (2012) argued for decentering the designer and for acknowledging the local, situated nature of design thinking. These revisions sought to keep the conceptual core of design thinking while also developing more effective approaches to deal with the shortcomings of standardized design thinking projects.

Moreover, the lack of structure in the design thinking process can make it difficult to evaluate from a practical standpoint. Suppositionally, design thinking promotes continual improvement—iterative cycles of design—which means designers work recursively to perfect a solution. Realistically, as experts have pointed out, it is not possible to ideate and test forever. Or, as Don Norman quipped, "It's time we started design doing. . . . it may be hard to come up with good ideas but it's even harder to actually do something with it, to produce a product" (Royal-Lawson & Axbom, 2016). Indeed, a solution needs to be implemented at some point, a reality that has been reflected in design thinking models that add a sixth phase focused specifically on implementation (Gibbons, 2016). Design thinking practitioners are challenged with this functional need in the commercial world. The necessity of implementation makes design thinking less of a rulebook (how to manage a project) than a lens for understanding users and the problems they face. Even within our own academic disciplinary practices, where the conventional mindset for addressing problems is to *invent solutions* with specific expectations for results (Jones et al., 2016), design thinking is difficult to deploy as a utopic schema for innovation. Like any other ways of seeing the world, *design thinking is a lens* for finding ways to address complex problems, and this lens has its benefits and limitations to various contexts. The teaching and application of design thinking, thus, require contextualization to best leverage its value.

Another strand of criticism emphasized more fundamental flaws in design thinking by describing it as a colonial approach. For example, Anoushka Khandwala (2019) argued that "to frame design thinking as a progressive narrative of global salvation ignores alternative ways of knowing" (n.p.). While numerous examples exist to support this claim, the most famous case is that of PlayPumps, which were covered by Amy Costello in two PBS *Frontline* stories. Essentially, PlayPumps replaced traditional hand pumps in several African nations with a merry-go-round style tool/toy that was intended to use children's play to pump water. When visiting the sites of several PlayPumps just a few years after they were installed, Costello found that they were not being used regularly and that many had already broken. Even more notably, local residents told Costello that they weren't consulted about the installation of the PlayPumps and that the devices were difficult for individual women to use (Costello, 2010, 10:45). In response to these kinds of flawed projects, there have been numerous calls to revise design thinking. For example, the liberatory design framework explicitly asks designers to reflect on how local histories of oppression impact their design projects (Anaissie et al., 2021). Amollo Ambole (2020) argued for decentering Western design paradigms in favor of the localized knowledge of African communities. Likewise, Chris Elawa (2016a, 2016b) advocated for replacing the Design For Africa paradigm with a Design In Africa approach that contributed to local communities' own design knowledge and capabilities. Finally, in conceptualizing a new Decolonial Design Thinking, Aishwarya Vardhana (2020) asked designers to center new questions in the design process:

> . . . how do we build technology that is revolutionary? Who is building the technology, where is it physically being built, and in what spirit? If imagination is rooted in experience, and technological innovation springs from imagination, from whose subjectivity are the technologies of today born? (n.p.)

Together, these kinds of approaches can help to revise the existing design thinking framework to support the goals of social justice and equity while also helping design projects respond better to the localized needs and knowledge of user communities.

▮ Design Thinking in Technical Communication

Now that we've discussed the practice broadly, we'd like to turn to situating design thinking specifically within TPC scholarship and pedagogy.

The field's interest in design thinking grows most directly out of the "design turn" in writing studies, popularized by Charles Kostelnick's (1989) alignment of design and writing at the peak of the field's process paradigm. Accordingly, the focus for design in TPC has been given to perceptual psychology (e.g., Moore & Fitz, 1993), visual rhetoric (Kostelnick, 1996; Tovey, 1996), user experience (Johnson, 1998; Sullivan, 1989) and usability studies (Breuch et al., 2001), multimodality (Wysocki, 2001), multiliteracies (Selber, 2004), information architecture (Salvo, 2004), and accessibility (Hitt, 2018; Melonçon, 2013), among others.

Amid this pluralistic approach to design in writing studies, the concept of design thinking recently entered TPC's discourse and literature. Stacked against existing frameworks, design thinking, as a ruthlessly user-centered, iterative invention process, emerges as a readily actionable scheme for TPC practices and instruction. Existing TPC scholarship has

- likened design thinking to the open-ended research in user experience design (Pflugfelder, 2017),
- situated design thinking as a rhetorical methodology (Greenwood et al., 2019),
- recommended positive deviance inquiries (or the study of rare but highly successful behaviors) as a tool for ideation, prototyping, and testing (Durá et al., 2019),
- explored the use of Dorst's problem framing approach for TPC work (Weedon, 2019),
- examined the connections between design thinking and place (Overmyer & Carlson, 2019),
- connected design thinking to content strategy (Zhou, 2020),
- demonstrated how a design thinking pedagogy could support TPC course outcomes (Bay et al., 2018; Lane, 2020; Pellegrini, 2021; Tham, 2021a, 2021b), and
- illustrated how a design thinking process could support the collaborative development of curricular design (Thominet, 2022).

Rebecca Pope-Ruark, Joe Moses, and Jason Tham (2019) have also developed a useful annotated bibliography of design thinking resources.

Beyond the connections to existing scholarship, there are several further reasons for TPC students to engage with design thinking. Despite the criticisms of it, design thinking remains a common strategy in a wide variety of industries and professions, including healthcare (Altman et al., 2018), information technology (Denning, 2013), and corporate writing (Moses & Tham, 2019). In this way, a foundation in design thinking practices can contribute to students' available tools to respond to existing industry trends.

Furthermore, there is good evidence that design thinking is often misapplied in practice, with the formalized d.school process applied as a rulebook rather than as a flexible, heuristic approach or lens (Greenwood et al., 2019). We hope that this book provides clarity to various components of the design thinking mindset so readers can understand it as a possible approach to solving problems in their own contexts. We believe that familiarity with design thinking could help students enter the workplace as experts ready to contribute to production and design.

Finally, as TPC continues to work to improve the inclusivity of our scholarship, pedagogy, and practice, we can draw on our existing expertise in user experience design and participatory design to contribute to efforts in reshaping design thinking practice as a localized, community-led process.

■ The Goal of the *Keywords* Collection

Given the discussions above, including the numerous formulations of the design thinking process as well as the ongoing work to revise and improve the process, it is clear that we have not established a firm understanding of design thinking even when it shows tremendous potential for shaping the work of technical communication. At the core of this concern is the absence of shared definitions, meanings, and processes that would warrant consistency in the pursuit of design thinking. With a majority of TPC students now entering an expanding profession where design thinking is routinely exercised, the time is right for an authoritative resource at the intersection of design thinking and technical communication to address these issues.

As scholar-teachers grapple with design thinking, and as students work to understand its principles and mechanisms, we need a lexical resource for grounding and clarification of design thinking in technical communication. Specifically, we need an inventory and analysis of the central terms in design thinking through the lens of technical communication to study how a given term circulates and affects our particular knowledge community. This collection is born of such exigency, and it begins that journey by inviting scholarly perspectives to which particular keywords in design thinking are conceptualized, applied, and studied in the context of technical communication.

This collection follows on the heels of cultural theorist Raymond Williams. In his landmark work *Keywords: A Vocabulary of Culture and Society* (1976), Williams demonstrated the value of a critical glossary in introducing established as well as emerging terms to readers of a particular field. Williams' pioneering collection has become a model to many disciplines, including language and literacy (Carter, 1995), creative writing (Bishop & Starkey, 2006), news and journalism (Zelizer & Allan, 2010), sound studies (Novak & Sakakeeny, 2015), travel writing (Forsdick et al., 2019), and our very own—composition/writing studies (Heilker & Vandenberg, 1996; 2015) and technical communication practices (Gallon, 2016).

Each of these volumes has explored principal ideas in a specific knowledge field. Over time, they also reveal the *ideals* and *realities* in a field based on its evolving lexicon. Paul Heilker and Peter Vandenberg's *Keywords in Writing Studies* (2015), a sequel to their *Keywords in Composition Studies* (1996), has traced the shifting theoretical, educational, professional, and institutional developments across a span of two decades. Ray Gallon's *The Language of Technical Communication* (2016) has sought to accomplish a similar goal: to predict the future of the field by defining what it is doing at the present. Essentially, keywords projects can provide for their respective disciplines an important point of intersection where the now meets the next. For scholars and practitioners alike, this intersection can serve as a departure to critical inquiry and prospective application.

Keywords in Design Thinking is a collaborative effort to clarify the language and concepts used to discuss design-centric practices in technical communication. This edited collection is designed for

- TPC students using or studying design thinking processes,
- researchers interested in using design thinking methodologies in their work,
- instructors working to augment their pedagogies with design thinking methodologies and activities, and
- program administrators and faculty wishing to draw programmatic connections between design thinking and TPC curricula.

The goal of this collection is to set the stage for design thinking within technical communication at a time when design thinking is itself deemed a contested term by many. It does so by establishing definitions stable enough to allow readers to determine the value of design thinking and apply and examine its usefulness in the design of technical communication. The contributors to this collection include faculty at research and comprehensive colleges, graduate students, and industry practitioners. This intentional configuration of contributors aims to increase the diversity of perspectives and offer varying routes to understanding design thinking.

■ The Design of the Collection

The most difficult task in curating this collection was the selection of keywords for inclusion. The initial call for this project was shared on numerous social media outlets and had garnered favorable responses from many interested contributors. Upon consultation with The WAC Clearinghouse Foundations and Innovations in Technical and Professional Communication series editors, 30 keywords (including **design thinking** in this introduction) were accepted for this collection based on their relevance and significance to the knowledge-building work this collection aims to achieve.

While it is almost an insurmountable task to justify the final selection, the 30 keywords in this collection have been carefully examined for their prevalence in the practice of design thinking and how they might inform technical communication. The primary objective of this collection is to present a set of keywords that would help readers not only to understand core design thinking methods but also the ways they may incorporate it in their own practices. Many of the selected keywords—like *creativity*, *innovation*, and *wicked problems*—have recurred in current scholarship. To bridge design thinking and commonplace technical communication concepts, technical keywords like *affordances*, *modularity*, *social design*, and *usability* were also deliberately included.

The final set of keywords includes the main phases of the design process, namely *empathy*, *problem definition*, *ideation*, *rapid prototyping*, *testing*, and *iteration*. To help readers see how they may apply design thinking in their respective contexts, the rest of the keywords include signature methods (e.g., *contextual inquiry*, *edge cases*, and *participatory design*), and concepts that help explicate the principles of design thinking (e.g., *collaboration*, *entrepreneurship*, and *inclusion*).

▪ Structure of the Chapters

Each keyword entry includes a definition and a synthesis of relevant research with examples to flesh out the keyword. To help readers navigate this collection, each entry contains the following sections:

1. Definition and background: Descriptions and useful contexts for the keyword
2. Design application: One or more exemplary applications of the keyword
3. Pedagogical integration: How the keyword may manifest in the TPC classroom
4. References and recommended readings: Resources to learn more about the keyword

As with the stylistic treatment demonstrated in this introduction, all cross-referenced keywords are bolded and called out in the individual entries.

▪ Open-Access Publication

Lastly, this collection is also born of a pressing desire to make knowledge accessible to public audiences. Modeled after innovative works like Guy McHenry's *Key Concepts in Surveillance Studies* (2017) and Cheryl Ball and Drew Loewe's *Bad Ideas About Writing* (2017), this collection is designed to be an open-access resource. Readers may reuse portions or all of this collection with basic attribution to the original texts and authors.

■ References

Altman, M., Huang, T. T. K. & Breland, J. Y. (2018). Design thinking in health care. *Preventing Chronic Disease, 15*, E117. https://doi.org/10.5888/pcd15.180128.

Ambole, A. (2020). Rethinking design making and design thinking in Africa. *Design and Culture, 12*(3), 331–350. https://doi.org/10.1080/17547075.2020.1788257.

Anaissie, T., Clifford, D., Wise, S. & The National Equity Project. (2021). *Liberatory design: Mindsets and modes to design for equity* [card deck]. https://www.liberatorydesign .com/ .

Ball, C. & Loewe, D. (Ed.). (2017). *Bad ideas about writing*. Digital Publishing Institute; West Virginia University Libraries. https://textbooks.lib.wvu.edu/badideas/badi-deasaboutwriting-book.pdf.

Bay, J., Johnson-Sheehan, R. & Cook, D. (2018). Design thinking via experiential learning: Thinking like an entrepreneur in technical communication courses. *Programmatic Perspectives, 10*(1), 172–200.

Bishop, W. & Starkey, D. (2006). *Keywords in creative writing*. Utah State University Press.

Breuch, L. A. K., Zachry, M. & Spinuzzi, C. (2001). Usability instruction in technical communication programs: New directions in curriculum development. *Journal of Business and Technical Communication, 15*(2), 223–240.

Brown, T. (2009). *Change by design: How design thinking transforms organizations and inspires innovation*. HarperBusiness.

Buchanan, R. (1992). Wicked problems in design thinking. *Design Issues, 8*(2), 5–21.

Carter, R. (1995). *Keywords in language and literacy*. Routledge.

Costello, A. (2010, June 29). Troubled water. *PBS Frontline*. https://www.pbs.org/video /frontlineworld-troubled-water/.

Cross, N. (1982). Designerly ways of knowing. *Design Studies, 3*(4), 221–227. https://doi .org/10.1016/0142-694X(82)90040-0.

Cross, N. (2001). Designerly ways of knowing: Design discipline versus design science. *Design Issues, 17*(3), 49–55. https://doi.org/10.1162/074793601750357196.

Cross, N. (2007). Forty years of design research. *Design Studies, 28*, 1–4. https://doi.org /10.1016/j.destud.2006.11.004.

d.school. (2010). *An introduction to design thinking: Process guide*. https://web.stanford. edu/~mshanks/MichaelShanks/files/509554.pdf.

Design Council (2019). The double diamond: A universally accepted depiction of the design process. https://www.designcouncil.org.uk/our-work/news-opinion/double -diamond-universally-accepted-depiction-design-process/.

Denning, P. J. (2013). Design thinking. *Communications of the ACM, 56*(12), 29–31. https:// doi.org/10.1145/2535915

Dorst, K. (2011). The core of 'design thinking' and its application. *Design Studies, 32*(6), 521–532. https://doi.org/10.1016/j.destud.2011.07.006.

Durá, L., Perez, L. & Chaparro, M. (2019). Positive deviance as design thinking: Challenging notions of stasis in technical and professional communication. *Journal of Business and Technical Communication, 33*(4), 376–399. https://doi.org/10.1177 /1050651919854057.

Elawa, C. (2016a, February 29). Stop designing for Africa. (Part 1). *Medium*. https:// medium.com/@chriselawa/stop-designing-for-africa-part-1-88331f8c2c3.

Elawa, C. (2016b, February 29). Stop designing for Africa. (Part 2). *Medium.* https://medium.com/@chriselawa/stop-designing-for-africa-part-2-ec7783badc09.

Forsdick, C., Kinsley, Z. & Walchester, K. (Eds.). (2019). *Keywords in travel writing studies: A critical glossary.* Anthem Press.

Fuller, R. B. (2019). *Utopia or oblivion: The prospects for humanity.* Lars Müller Publishers.

Gallon, R. (Ed.). (2016). *The language of technical communication.* XML Press.

Gibbons, S. (2016, July 31). *Design thinking 101.* Nielsen Norman Group. https://www.nngroup.com/articles/design-thinking/.

Greenwood, A., Lauren, B., Knott, J. & DeVoss, D. N. (2019). Dissensus, resistance, and ideology: Design thinking as a rhetorical methodology. *Journal of Business and Technical Communication, 33*(4), 400–424. https://doi.org/10.1177/1050651919854063.

Hackos, J. (1984). Teaching problem-solving strategies in the technical communication classroom. *IEEE Transactions for Professional Communication, 27*(4), 180–184.

Hackos, J. (1997). From theory to practice: Using the information process-maturity model as a tool for strategic planning. *Technical Communication, 44*(4), 369–380.

Hackos, J. & Redish, J. (1998). *User and task analyses for interface design.* Wiley Computer Publishing.

Heilker, P. & Vandenberg, P. (Eds.). (1996). *Keywords in composition studies.* Boynton/Cook Publishers.

Heilker, P. & Vandenberg, P. (Eds.). (2015). *Keywords in writing studies.* Utah State University Press.

Hitt, A. (2018). Foregrounding accessibility through (inclusive) universal design in professional communication curricula. *Business and Professional Communication Quarterly, 81*(1), 52–65.

IBM. (2018). *Enterprise design thinking field guide.* https://www.ibm.com/cloud/garage/content/field-guide/design-thinking-field-guide/.

IDEO. (2015). *The field guide to human-centered design.* http://www.designkit.org/resources/1

Interaction Design Foundation. (n.d.). Design thinking: A non-linear process. https://public-media.interaction-design.org/images/uploads/34a545643d169a37480de10b731fb6df.jpeg.

Johnson, R. R. (1998). *User-centered technology: A rhetorical theory for computers and other mundane things.* SUNY Press.

Johnson-Eilola, J. & Selber, S. (2013). *Solving problems in technical communication.* University of Chicago Press.

Jones, N. N., Moore, K. R. & Walton, R. (2016). Disrupting the past to disrupt the future: An antenarrative of technical communication. *Technical Communication Quarterly, 25*(4), 211–229.

Kelley, T. & Littman, J. (2001). *The art of innovation: Lessons in creativity from IDEO, America's leading design firm.* Doubleday.

Khandwala, A. (2019, June 5). What does it mean to decolonize design? *AIGA Eye on Design.* https://eyeondesign.aiga.org/what-does-it-mean-to-decolonize-design/.

Kimbell, L. (2011). Rethinking design thinking: Part I. *Design and Culture, 3*(3), 285–306. https://doi.org/10.2752/175470811X13071166525216.

Kimbell, L. (2012). Rethinking design thinking: Part II. *Design and Culture, 4*(2), 129–148. https://doi.org/10.2752/175470812X13281948975413.

Kostelnick, C. (1989). Process paradigm in design and composition: Affinities and directions. *College Composition and Communication, 40*(3), 267–281.

Kostelnick, C. (1996). Supra-textual design: The visual rhetoric of whole documents. *Technical Communication Quarterly, 5*(1), 9–33.

Lane, L. (2020). Interstitial design processes: How design thinking and social design processes bridge theory and practice in TPC pedagogy. In M. J. Klein (Ed.), *Effective teaching of technical communication: Theory, practice, and application* (pp. 29–43). The WAC Clearinghouse; University Press of Colorado. https://doi.org/10.37514/TPC-B .2020.1121.2.02.

Liedtka, J., King, A. & Bennett, K. (2013). *Solving problems with design thinking: Ten stories of what works.* Columbia University Press.

McHenry, G. (Ed.). (2017). *Key concepts in surveillance studies.* https://surveillancestudies .pressbooks.com/ .

Melonçon, L. (Ed.). (2013). *Rhetorical accessAbility: At the intersection of technical communication and disability studies.* Baywood Publishing.

Moore, P. & Fitz, C. (1993). Using Gestalt theory to teach document design and graphics. *Technical Communication Quarterly, 4,* 389–410.

Moses, J. & Tham, J. (2019, March 25). Is design thinking the key to your next corporate writing gig? *Medium.* https://joemoses004.medium.com/is-design-thinking-the-key -to-your-next-corporate-writing-gig-abf8e23436b2.

Novak, D. & Sakakeeny, M. (Eds.). (2015). *Keywords in sound.* Duke University Press.

Nussbaum, B. (2011). Design thinking is a failed experiment. So what's next? *Fast Company.* https://www.fastcompany.com/1663558/design-thinking-is-a-failed-experiment -so-whats-next.

Overmyer, T. & Carlson, E. B. (2019). Literature review: Design thinking and place. *Journal of Business and Technical Communication, 33*(4), 431–436. https://doi.org/10 .1177/1050651919854079.

Pellegrini, M. (2022). Composing like an entrepreneur: The pedagogical implications of design thinking in the workplace. *Journal of Technical Writing and Communication, 52*(3), 316–333. https://doi.org/10.1177/00472816211031554.

Pflugfelder, E. (2017). Methodologies: Design studies and techne. In L. Potts & M. J. Salvo (Eds.), *Rhetoric and experience architecture* (pp. 166–183). Parlor Press.

Pope-Ruark, R. (2019). Design thinking in technical and professional communication: Four perspectives. *Journal of Business and Technical Communication, 33*(4), 437–455. https://doi.org/10.1177/1050651919854094.

Pope-Ruark, R., Moses, J. & Tham, J. (2019). Iterating the literature: An early annotated bibliography of design-thinking resources. *Journal of Business and Technical Communication, 33*(4), 456–465. https://doi.org/10.1177/1050651919854096.

Rittel, H. W. J. & Webber, M. M. (1973). Dilemmas in a general theory of planning. *Policy Sciences, 4*(2), 155–169.

Rowe, P. G. (1987). *Design thinking.* MIT Press.

Royal-Lawson, J. & Axbom, P. (2016). Design doing with Don Norman (No. 125). [Audio podcast episode].In *UX Podcast.* https://medium.com/@uxpodcast/design-doing -with-don-norman-6434b02283ib.

Salvo, M. (2004). Rhetorical action in professional space: Information architecture as critical practice. *Journal of Business and Technical Communication, 18*(1), 39–66.

Schön, D. A. (1983). *The reflective practitioner: How professionals think in action.* Basic Books.

Seelig, T. (2015). Insight out: Get ideas out of your head and into the world. HarperOne.

Selber, S. (2004). *Multiliteracies for a digital age*. Southern Illinois University Press.

Simon, H. A. (1996). *The sciences of the artificial*. MIT Press.

Sullivan, P. (1989). Beyond a narrow conception of usability testing. *IEEE Transactions on Professional Communication, 32*(4), 256–264.

Sutton, R. I. & Hoyt, D. (2016, January 6). Better service, faster: A design thinking case study. *Harvard Business Review*. https://hbr.org/2016/01/better-service-faster-a -design-thinking-case-study.

Tham, J. (2021a). *Design thinking in technical communication: Solving problems through making and collaboration*. Routledge.

Tham, J. (2021b). Engaging design thinking and making in technical and professional communication pedagogy. *Technical Communication Quarterly, 30*(4), 392–409. https:// doi.org/10.1080/10572252.2020.1804619.

Thominet, L. (2022). Ideating a new program: Implementing design thinking approaches to develop program student learning outcomes. In K. Crane & K. Cargile Cook (Eds.), *User experience as innovative academic practice* (pp. 161–195). The WAC Clearinghouse; University Press of Colorado. https://doi.org/10.37514/TPC-B.2022 .1367.2.01.

Tovey, J. (1996). Computer interfaces and visual rhetoric: Looking at the technology. *Technical Communication Quarterly, 5*(1), 61–76.

Vardhana, A. (2020, November 11). Decolonial design thinking. *Medium*. https:// medium.com/carre4/decolonial-design-thinking-9eee3071c33d.

Vinsel, L. (2018, May 21). Design thinking is a boondoggle. *Chronicle of Higher Education*. https://www.chronicle.com/article/design-thinking-is-a-boondoggle/.

Weedon, S., Pope-Ruark, R., Tham, J., Moses, J. & Conner, T. (2019). The core of Kees Dorst's design thinking: A literature review. *Journal of Business & Technical Communication, 33*(4), 425–430. https://doi.org/10.1177/1050651919854077.

Williams, R. (1976). *Keywords: A vocabulary of culture and society*. Croom Helm.

Wysocki, A. F. (2001). Impossibly distinct: On form/content and word/image in two pieces of computer-based interactive multimedia. *Computers and Composition, 18*(2), 137–162.

Zelizer, B. & Allan, S. (2010). *Keywords in news and journalism studies*. McGraw Hill; Open University Press.

Zhou, Q. (2020). Building design thinking into content strategy. *Proceedings of the 38th ACM International Conference on Design of Communication*, 1–5. https://doi.org/10 .1145/3380851.3416738.

Part 1: The Design Thinking Phases

▌ 1. Empathy

Scott Wible
University of Maryland, College Park

▌ Definition and Background

The first principle of design thinking is empathy. Social work scholar Brené Brown defines empathy as "the emotional skill set that allows us to understand what someone is experiencing" as well as "to recognize and understand another person's emotions" (2021, pp. 120–121). Empathizing with users requires designers to be conscious of their own preconceived notions and biases in order to listen and observe "with a truly open mind" how users live and make sense of their day-to-day lives (Kelley with Littman, 2005, p. 17). In other words, empathy doesn't mean just thinking, "Here's how I would feel in that person's situation," but rather requires acknowledging and respecting those different experiences and perspectives.

Empathy research is critical for effective design thinking practice. By immersing themselves in the context of users' lives, designers gain insights that enable them to define problems or opportunities from their potential users' perspective and, in turn, to develop solutions that reflect users' values, fit the contexts of their lives, and will be more likely to be adopted by and ultimately benefit users.

Design thinkers are not only concerned with what they observe people do but also ask questions that prompt users to uncover the thoughts and emotions motivating their actions (Dam & Siang, 2020). For example, when the U.S. Department of Veteran Affairs (VA) Center for Innovation wanted to better understand "the experiences Veterans and their families have when attempting to access mental healthcare" (2016, p. 12), they talked at length with over five dozen Veterans—a diverse group across military branches and ranks as well as across gender, race, class, age, and geographic differences—their family members, and both frontline VA and private-sector service providers. By listening to their stories, the VA came "to better understand the processes and pathways people undergo to gain mentally healthy lives" and "gained a rich picture of their frustrations and aspirations" concerning mental health care (2016, p. 12).

▌ Design Application

Empathic design is grounded in ***contextual inquiry***, which involves observing and listening to how people live and make meaning within the material and social spaces of their lives (Leonard & Rayport, 1997). For example, when the New York

DOI: https://doi.org/10.37514/TPC-B.2022.1725.2.01

City Mayor's Office of Digital Strategy wanted to better understand how New Yorkers engage with municipal services through their digital devices, they did not distribute general surveys or convene focus groups in a meeting room. Instead, working with design specialists at the nonprofit Public Policy Lab, they got out of their offices in City Hall and met with a diverse range of residents, particularly disadvantaged populations such as those who have mental health issues or physical disabilities, are socially isolated, have low literacy skills, do not read or speak English, or are very low income. To gain empathy for these users, the designers observed how they attempt to access city services, whether digitally or in person, and they prompted them to talk about what they were thinking and how they were feeling before, during, and after these experiences (Public Policy Lab, 2016).

Uses NYCHA website to pay rent. Takes kids to library; uses library computer when there. **DO**	Wants more control over when rent is due each month. **THINK**
SAY "Private companies do a better job securing my financial data." "I have to enter all of my personal information every single month."	**FEEL** Doesn't fully trust government with security of her data. Frustrated that the NYCHA website doesn't recognize her month to month.

Figure 1.1. An empathy map for a low-income mother's experience with New York City's digital services. Image created by Wible, adapted from empathy research data in Public Policy Lab (2016).

Empathy mapping is one tool designers use to analyze and synthesize the data they collect through empathy interviews and observations (Dam & Siang, 2021). First, design teams use a technique called Story Share & Capture, in which they read through their notes and isolate key words or phrases from the interviews, usually by transcribing them with markers and sticky notes (Interaction Design Foundation). Next, designers arrange these notes on their "map," which is a 2x2 grid with the following four quadrants (such as Figure 1.1):

- What the person *says* (that is, memorable quotes)
- What the person *does* (or says that they do)
- What the person *thinks*
- What the person *feels*

Designers can either create a separate empathy map for each person they interview, or they can layer their notes onto the same map, ideally using different colors of sticky notes to distinguish the different people they've interviewed. Then, designers group similar keywords and phrases within the different quadrants of their empathy map, looking to identify clusters of concerns or problems that different users encounter in a similar way, particularly in terms of how they think or feel about their experiences.

Designers can also create a user journey map as a means to analyze their empathy research (Komninos & Briggs, 2021). Here, designers map major phases of the user experience and then layer their user empathy map notes about what users do, say, think, and feel into those different parts of the user journey. This analytical tool can help designers to identify specific moments where users experience problems that serve as opportunities for designers.

Empathy and journey mapping, then, help designers to keep their users' experience at the center of their problem definition and solution development work.

◼ Pedagogical Integration

In technical communication classes, students can practice empathy mapping as a way of understanding users. For example, my students engaged in design work aimed at helping the university create solutions to better support first-year faculty. To gain empathy with new faculty, students observed them in a wide range of contexts, including familiar settings such as classrooms and office hours, as well as labs, weekly research team meetings, and walks to and from campus. Students also asked new faculty to tell stories about their experiences during their first days, weeks, and semester on campus, using prompts such as "Tell me about a day when you left campus feeling energized and excited to work here" or "Describe a time when you left campus feeling frustrated and like you never wanted to come back."

A student group that interviewed several first-year science faculty noticed that many of them described feelings of "loneliness," "isolation," and "lacking community" as they struggled to set up their new research teams. Clustering these repeated and related keywords on their empathy map helped the student-designers to focus their problem definition on these deeper, conflicted emotional experiences of first-year science faculty. Creating an empathy map helped these student-designers to understand how faculty's stories about their experiences revealed their deeper thoughts and feelings, and the students then used these insights to focus their **problem definition** in a way that reflected faculty's experiences and needs.

■ References and Recommended Readings

Brown, B. (2021). *Atlas of the heart: Mapping meaningful connection and the language of human experience*. Random House.

Chapman, M. (2016, May 27). Designing beyond empathy. *Medium*. https://medium.com/ideo-stories/designing-beyond-empathy–2379865322fb.

Dam, R. F. & Siang, T. Y. (2020). *What is empathy and why is it so important in design thinking?*. Interaction Design Foundation. https://www.interaction-design.org/literature/article/design-thinking-getting-started-with-empathy.

Dam, R. F. & Siang, T. Y. (2021). *Empathy map: Why and how to use it*. Interaction Design Foundation. https://www.interaction-design.org/literature/article/empathy-map-why-and-how-to-use-it.

Etches, A. (2013). Know thy users: User research techniques to build empathy and improve decision-making. *Accidental Technologist, 53*(1), 13–17.

Interaction Design Foundation. (n.d.). *Story share and capture*. https://public-media.interaction-design.org/pdf/Story-Share-and-Capture.pdf.

Kelley, T., with Littman, J. (2005). *The ten faces of innovation*. Doubleday.

Kolko, J. (2010). Abductive thinking and sensemaking: The drivers of design synthesis. *Design Issues, 26*(1), 15–28.

Komninos, A. & Briggs, C. (2021). *Customer journey maps: Walking a mile in your customer's shoes*. Interaction Design Foundation. https://www.interaction-design.org/literature/article/customer-journey-maps-walking-a-mile-in-your-customer-s-shoes.

Leake, E. (2016). Writing pedagogies of empathy: As rhetoric and disposition. *Composition Forum, 34*. https://compositionforum.com/issue/34/empathy.php.

Leonard, D. & Rayport, J. F. (1997). Spark innovation through empathic design. *Harvard Business Review, 75*(6), 102.

Public Policy Lab. (2016). *New Yorkers' digital service needs: Findings from discovery research for the NYC Digital Playbook*. https://www.publicpolicylab.org/projects/.

Thomas, J. & McDonagh, D. (2013). Empathic design: Research strategies. *Australasian Medical Journal, 6*(1), 1–6.

VA Center for Innovation and the Public Policy Lab. (2016). Veteran access to mental health services: Current experiences and future design opportunities to better serve veterans and front-line providers. http://publicpolicylab.org/projects/veteran-mental-health/.

Walton, R. E. (2016). Supporting human dignity and human rights: A call to adopt the first principle of human-centered design. *Journal of Technical Writing and Communication, 46*(4), 402–426.

2. Problem Definition

Scott Wible
UNIVERSITY OF MARYLAND, COLLEGE PARK

Definition and Background

Design thinkers aim to create innovative solutions for users, but truly innovative problem-solving only starts with a clear, focused, insightful definition of the user's problem. The second phase of design thinking, problem definition, is the process of translating insights from user research into meaningful and actionable statements.

As they carry out *empathy* research about users' experiences, design thinkers go broad, expanding and deepening their contextual understanding of user experiences in all their complexity (see *wicked problems*). Designers then use analytical techniques such as empathy mapping and journey mapping in order to narrow their focus, generate insights about users' experiences, and define the specific user problem they will try to solve. Design thinkers frame the problem statement from the perspective or vantage point of the user or community for whom they are designing. That is, the problem definition should be cast in terms of keyword clusters that emerged during empathy mapping—"saying," "doing," "thinking," and "feeling" words and phrases from the designer's observation of user actions and interviews with stakeholders. Drawing on one's empathy research in this way can ensure the problem statement includes a unique insight about the user's context-specific experiences or needs.

Framing a problem statement is challenging but critically important (see experiences of scholars working on problem definition in Cooke et al., 2020; Tham, 2021; and Wible, 2020). Define a problem too narrowly, and it will constrain the solutions that designers feel free to generate in their *ideation* and *prototyping*; frame the problem too broadly or vaguely, however, and the designer's not likely to be creating a solution that addresses the user's deeply rooted problems or that captures a potential design opportunity. Design thinkers often draft several different problem statements in order to shed light on different aspects of the users' experiences—and perhaps even to focus on different types of users—and this experimentation can help design thinkers to see, early on, which problem definitions energize their ideation in the most vigorous ways. Problem definition also highlights the iterative nature of design thinking, for designers might generate insights through prototype testing that lead them to revise their definition of the user's problem in new ways.

Design Application

One useful tool for framing a problem definition is called a point-of-view (POV) statement (Cross, 2011). A POV statement offers an abductive-reasoning approach

DOI: https://doi.org/10.37514/TPC-B.2022.1725.2.02

to unpack puzzling situations. Design theorist Kees Dorst (2011) argued that "it may be strategic to temporarily suspend the generation of 'rich' descriptions of design and instead take a 'sparse' account as [the] starting point" (p. 522), but more importantly, designers need "strategies to tackle the complex creative challenge coming up with both a 'thing' and its 'working principle' that are linked to the attainment of a certain value" (p. 524). Dorst (2011) presented the following frame of abduction, shown in Figure 2.1.

Since design thinking is first and foremost a human-centered methodology, POV statements replace the "thing" (what) with actual user personas (who) in the abductive reasoning situation to guide designers in framing a problem that focuses on what users need and value. Typically, POV statements take the templated shape shown in Figure 2.2.

Figure 2.3 shows an example of a POV statement created by professional writing students working to improve the experience of first-year faculty on campus.

There are three important tasks to keep in mind in crafting an effective POV statement with this template. First, write the POV statement from the perspective of the user, reflecting the user's experiences, perspectives, values, and language; consequently, good problem definitions only take shape after empathy research and never at the very beginning of the design thinking process when the designer only has their own ideas and hunches about what the problem is.

Second, define the need using verbs, not nouns. Put a slightly different way, problem definition should not include the solution (the noun) in it, for that would severely constrain—indeed, even eliminate the need for—a designer's ideation. Instead, the POV statement should be crafted in a way to focus on the ideal end goal that the user should be able to achieve or experience (the verb) with any new solution.

WHAT + HOW *leads to* **VALUE**
FRAME

Figure 2.1. Dorst's (2011) abductive reasoning frame.

Name and brief description of user **(Who)**

needs a way to

do X **(How)**

because, surprisingly,

insight from empathy research **(Value)**.

Figure 2.2. A template for writing POV statements.

> Nathalie, a new biology professor starting her own research lab for the first time
>
> ## needs a way to
>
> experience connection and companionship with other researchers on campus,
>
> ## because, surprisingly,
>
> she has felt "academic loneliness" since stepping on campus and not immediately joining an already vibrant, communal research team.

Figure 2.3. A sample POV statement.

Third, incorporate a surprising insight from the ***empathy*** research and empathy mapping, particularly those deep insights about how a user thinks or feels about their experiences, as these insights too often get overlooked or ignored in favor of more material needs and ***constraints*** that users experience.

While designers should be guided by their problem definition as they work through the stages of brainstorming and developing solutions, they should also know that a problem definition statement should not be seen as finished once it's first composed. During ***ideation***, for example, a design team might discover that the problem statement has been crafted either too narrowly or too broadly to focus brainstorming in productive ways. Or, as designers are ***testing*** their solution prototypes with users, they might discover unique insights about users' experiences or perspectives that add nuance and depth to—or perhaps even radically redirect—the problem definition.

■ Pedagogical Integration

While problem definition may seem parallel to the formation of a research problem in conventional TPC pedagogy, the design thinking approach requires students to employ a continuous questioning that differs from a linear progressive manner to the characterization of problems. To foster a design thinking mindset, instructors may encourage students to create a preliminary framing of the problem using the POV statement exercise. For example:

> Let's say you are working to help senior (older) users attend online courses. You have observed a few users and spoken to them about their online learning experience, and you've learned about some of their struggles.
>
> Read the following persona that emerged from your empathy research:
>
> "Maggie Smith is a retired U.S. Air Force lieutenant colonel. She has been spending a lot of time at home since retirement and would

like to participate in local nonprofit organizing efforts using her expertise in finance and accounting. However, she realized there's a plethora of new accounting software that she needs to learn in order to help her local organizations. She found out there are free online courses she can take through providers like edX, Udacity, and Coursera, but it has been a difficult experience for her to navigate those websites. She is particularly frustrated by the confusing course modules and assignment requirements. She would like to see a more straightforward structure in these online courses."

Use the template presented in this chapter to write a POV statement for Maggie.

Guided by the user requirement enlightened in the POV statement, students can formulate an initial set of design questions that would serve as an anchor to their innovation process. Given the iterative nature of design thinking, students should revisit the definition of the problem in every design review and project update meeting so they may align their effort with the exigency (i.e., need and motivation) of the project. To revisit their problem definition, students should consider a regular debrief meeting that examines the alignment of their empathy research, problem statements, and solution development, asking questions such as "What have we done so far to address the problem? That step hasn't been done, and what needs to be done?" Later in the design thinking process, as students test their prototypes with users, they should use these debrief meetings to ask, "What new empathy insights have we discovered that prompt us to see our problem definition in a new light?"

■ References and Recommended Readings

Cooke, L., Dusenberry, L. & Robinson, J. (2020). Gaming design thinking: Wicked problems, sufficient solutions, and the possibility space of games. *Technical Communication Quarterly*, *29*(4), 327–340.

Cross, N. (2011). *Design thinking: Understanding how designers think and work*. Bloomsbury Publishing.

Dorst, K. (2011). The core of 'design thinking' and its application. *Design Studies*, *32*(6), 521–532.

Gregersen, H. (2018). *Questions are the answer: A breakthrough approach to your most vexing problems at work and life*. Harper.

Kelley, T. & Kelley, D. (2013). Spark: From blank page to insight. In T. Kelly & D. Kelly (Eds.), *Creative confidence: Unleashing the creative potential within us all* (pp. 67–107). Crown.

Kolko, J. (2010). Abductive thinking and sensemaking: The drivers of design synthesis. *Design Issues*, *26*(1), 15–28.

Lewrick, M., Link, P. & Leifer, L. (2018a). How to find the right focus. In M. Lewrick, P. Link & L. Leifer (Eds.), *The design thinking playbook: Mindful digital transformation of teams, products, services, businesses and ecosystems* (pp. 80–89). Wiley.

Lewrick, M., Link, P. & Leifer, L. (2018b). How to get a good problem statement. In
    M. Lewrick, P. Link & L. Leifer (Eds.), *The design thinking playbook: Mindful digital
    transformation of teams, products, services, businesses and ecosystems* (pp. 50–58). Wiley.
Paton, B. & Dorst, K. (2011). Briefing and reframing: A situated practice. *Design Studies,
    32*(6), 573–587.
Tham, J. (2021). Engaging design thinking and making in technical and professional
    communication pedagogy. *Technical Communication Quarterly, 30*(4), 392–409. https://
    doi.org/10.1080/10572252.2020.1804619.
Wible, S. (2020). Using design thinking to teach creative problem solving in writing
    courses. *College Composition and Communication, 71*(3), 339–425.

3. Ideation

Jennifer Sano-Franchini
WEST VIRGINIA UNIVERSITY

■ Definition and Background

Ideation, or idea generation, is a key moment—or series of moments—in the design process where an individual or group takes steps to generate ideas relevant to their design. Ideation may involve a number of practices and strategies used for creative production, including brainstorming, sketching, and **rapid prototyping**. In addition, ideation can occur at various parts of a nonlinear and recursive design process, whether for better understanding the complex dimensions of a **wicked problem** or coming up with possible design solutions. Although it is not often historicized in contemporary usage, the term *ideation* and its variants *ideate* and *ideational* have been in use in the English language since at least the 1800s (the 1600s, in the case of *ideate*). At times understood in contradistinction to sensation, ideation has been used as a way of discussing creativity and the thinking process, as well as psychology and how the human brain works. In more recent decades, ideation has been studied and applied in disciplines ranging from social and organizational psychology, engineering, architecture, management, entrepreneurship, and user experience and technology design (see, for instance: Baruah & Paulus, 2011; Basadur et al., 1982; Bradner et al., 2014; Cullen, 2013; Gundry et al., 2016; Hay et al., 2019; Shah et al., 2003). From a design thinking perspective, ideation is often understood as "the process of generating a broad set of ideas on a given topic, with no attempt to judge or evaluate them" (Harley, 2017a), and it tends to include several common features:

- First, a time limit is set. Ideation sessions often last between 15 minutes and an hour, depending on the group dynamic and the complexity of the problem.
- Second, one or more designated facilitators pose a prompt or series of questions to guide ideation.
- Next, quantity is prioritized over quality. The more ideas the better.
- To amass this large quantity of ideas, participants must withhold judgment. No idea is too out there. Instead, wild and divergent thinking is encouraged. This step is based on the understanding that evaluation can stifle creativity.
- In a group ideation session in particular, participants should work in **collaboration** with one another, building from the ideas of others. To do so, participants must actively and openly consider the ideas of others. This principle is based on the understanding that collaboration enables the

DOI: https://doi.org/10.37514/TPC-B.2022.1725.2.03

generation of diverse ideas, which is key to ***creativity***. That said, the open inclusion of diverse perspectives within an organization can enable a particularly productive ideation session (McLeod & Lobel, 1992).

- Finally, the ideas are recorded and the session is documented (Harley, 2017b).

While these are features that are common in ideation, especially in UX contexts, there are many variations in tools and techniques that are used to ideate. Ideation sessions often involve the use of analog tools—whiteboard and dry erase markers, flipchart paper and markers, post-its and pens—but they can also involve the use of digital tools, such as Google Docs, Miro, Lucidchart, and other concept mapping technologies.

In addition to enabling the possibility of considering a diverse range of ideas, ideation provides a set of strategies for creativity and unconventional thinking—qualities that are important for successful technical and professional communication. As Haakon Faste et al. (2013) suggested, the value of ideation may be less about "the generation of novel ideas than the cultural influence exerted by unconventional ideas on the ideating team" (p. 1343). Further, ideation can get people to start talking when they may be reluctant to do so, and thus strengthen community bonds within the team.

With these affordances in mind, it is important to note some potential limitations of ideation practices as related to equity, inclusion, and accessibility. For instance, some have argued that depending on the guidelines presented, ideation can be set up such that extroverts dominate, and as Cynthia Bennett et al. (2016) asserted, ideation is often carried out in ways that are not accessible for people with disabilities. They explain, "many students are taught to ideate by sketching, but this method may be difficult for people with vision or mobility impairments" (Bennett et al., 2016, p. 303). In addition, d/Deaf or hard of hearing individuals may be excluded from common ideation practices that involve frequent verbal interruptions among a large group of people. Bennett et al. (2016) reported that such participants "expressed frustration lip reading or watching an interpreter during a fast-paced conversation while also examining sketches or other artifacts" (p. 303). It is thus imperative that we attend to accessibility in ideation, by considering the experiences and positionalities of all participants within a given context, and by designing accessible mechanisms accordingly, whether for slowing down, highlighting points of synthesis, making space for all participants to contribute, and/or encouraging the use of multiple modes of communication—the visual, the aural, and the tactile.

■ Design Application

There are numerous techniques used to guide ideation and to encourage the generation of new, creative, and viable ideas (Smith, 1998). For example, Noe

Vargas Hernandez et al. (2010) identified several common ideation methods, including:

- use of "provocative stimuli," which involves presenting participants with related and unrelated images, objects, sounds, and other stimuli as a way of eliciting new ideas;
- "frame of reference shifting," or "[changing] how objects and requirements are being viewed, perceived, interpreted";
- "example exposure," or providing an example solution to the problem as a way of exciting ideas; and
- "incubation," or adding a programmed delay "to allow sub-conscious processing to take place" (p. 387).

When can ideation take place? Often, it occurs after *problem definition* and after having some understanding of users. For example, once a design problem has been identified and after user research has taken place, a team might come together to ideate possible solutions to the problem that are appropriate for users. At the same time, ideation can also be used earlier in the design process, for problem definition. That is, if an organization wanted to improve its protocols or if they wanted to contribute to solving a "wicked" social problem, they might bring people together to ideate the range of problems for potential consideration.

To provide one example among these many possibilities of ideation in the context of technical and professional communication, a technical writer—or group of writers—working to develop user documentation might begin by considering the problem(s) the documentation is meant to address, whether that be user navigation of a specific technology, the difficulties users might experience when troubleshooting particular technical problems, or accessibility of that technical document itself. They might then research who their users are, speaking with diverse users and asking questions meant to elicit an understanding of how users experience that technology or document. Then, with those problems and understandings of user experience in mind, the technical communicator or technical communication team might ideate a hundred solutions that would enhance accessibility and user experience, before reviewing and narrowing down those solutions to identify those that would best address the problem(s) at hand.

For group sessions in particular, it is helpful to designate a facilitator who provides guidance and who is able to model what effective ideation looks like, reminding participants, as needed, to withhold judgment. The facilitator should encourage the consideration of creative possibilities, as well as demonstrate how to build off of one another's ideas, and should ensure that there is a clear record of the session. As noted in the previous section, the facilitator should also consider the *equity*, accessibility, and *social justice* related implications of ideation practices with their specific context and participants in mind. Finally, as an act of accountability, the facilitator should follow up with the team, letting them know how their ideas will be used as the project unfolds.

■ Pedagogical Integration

Ideation as a pedagogical practice can be especially helpful for encouraging students to think beyond the first viable idea that comes to mind, to help them recognize that there is value to taking the time to consider other possibilities, as there may be other more interesting and effective solutions for a given problem. Ideation can also be used to form groups based on student interests for collaborative projects. As an example, students may be asked to identify a number of wicked problems, before individually selecting the top five problems that are most compelling to them. In a course on feminism and interaction design, for instance, students might ideate 100 wicked problems related to feminism, ranging from the problem of sexual violence on college campuses, to sex trafficking, to attacks on people's right to safe and legal abortion (Sano-Franchini, 2017). Students can then indicate the top three to five problems they are most interested in addressing, and groups may then be formed on the basis of students' shared interests. I often ask students to come up with 100 problems, as it is a high enough number such that they need to think beyond what they might typically do for a class project, but not so high that it is impossible to accomplish within a single class session. This is one context where it is especially important for the instructor-facilitator to model for students what effective ideation can and should look like. Students can then work within their groups to ideate 100 possible solutions to the wicked problem that was the basis of their grouping.

Students may also learn and exercise ideation through low-stakes activities that encourage them to pursue unconventional ideas. The Stanford d.school (2018) design thinking orientation offers one model. In pairs, students first interview each other to understand the problem space or situation, as well as user needs. Then, under a time pressure (seven to eight minutes), students are challenged to sketch a handful of radical solutions without needing to account for the constraints of practicality or resource-related limitation. Next, students are asked to present their four to five sketches to their partner to gather initial reactions. Having gathered those responses, students spend another five minutes choosing one best idea from the sketches and refine it based on their partner's feedback. This learning exercise can be integrated into usability studies, user experience research, or general technical and professional communication pedagogies as a way to promote creativity.

■ References and Recommended Readings

Baruah, J. & Paulus, P. B. (2011). Category assignment and relatedness in the group ideation process. *Journal of Experimental Social Psychology, 47*(6), 1070–1077.

Basadur, M., Graen, G. B. & Green, S. G. (1982). Training in creative problem solving: Effects on ideation and problem finding and solving in an industrial research organization. *Organizational Behavior and Human Performance, 30*(1), 41–70.

Bennett, C. L., Shinohara, K., Blaser, B., Davidson, A. & Steele, K. M. (2016, October). Using a design workshop to explore accessible ideation. In *Proceedings of the 18th International ACM SIGACCESS Conference on Computers and Accessibility* (pp. 303–304).

Bradner, E., Iorio, F. & Davis, M. (2014, April). Parameters tell the design story: Ideation and abstraction in design optimization. In *Proceedings of the Symposium on Simulation for Architecture and Urban Design* (p. 26).

Cullen, J. G. (2013). Vocational ideation and management career development. *Journal of Management Development, 32*(9), 932–944.

Dam, R. & Siang, T. (2018a). *Stage 3 in the design thinking process: Ideate.* Interaction Design Foundation. https://www.interaction-design.org/literature/article/stage-3 -in-the-design-thinking-process-ideate

Dam, R. & Siang, T. (2018b). *What is ideation—and how to prepare for ideation sessions.* Interaction Design Foundation. https://www.interaction-design.org/literature /article/what-is-ideation-and-how-to-prepare-for-ideation-sessions.

Faste, H., Rachmel, N., Essary, R. & Sheehan, E. (2013, April). Brainstorm, chainstorm, cheatstorm, tweetstorm: New ideation strategies for distributed HCI design. In *Proceedings of the SIGCHI Conference on Human Factors in Computing Systems* (pp. 1343–1352).

Gundry, L. K., Ofstein, L. F. & Monllor, J. (2016). Entrepreneurial team creativity: Driving innovation from ideation to implementation. *Journal of Enterprising Culture, 24*(1), 55–77.

Harley, A. (2017a). *Ideation for everyday design challenges.* Nielsen Norman Group. https://www.nngroup.com/articles/ux-ideation/.

Harley, A. (2017b). *Ideation in practice: How effective UX teams generate ideas.* Nielsen Norman Group. https://www.nngroup.com/articles/ideation-in-practice/.

Hay, L., Duffy, A. H., Gilbert, S. J., Lyall, L., Campbell, G., Coyle, D. & Grealy, M. A. (2019). The neural correlates of ideation in product design engineering practitioners. *Design Science, 5*, E29, 1–23.

Hernandez, N. V., Shah, J. J. & Smith, S. M. (2010). Understanding design ideation mechanisms through multilevel aligned empirical studies. *Design Studies, 31*(4), 382–410.

Ideation. Interaction Design Foundation. https://www.interaction-design.org/literature /topics/ideation.

McLeod, P. L. & Lobel, S. A. (1992). The effects of ethnic diversity on idea generation in small groups. *Academy of Management Best Papers Proceedings,* 227–231.

Sano-Franchini, J. (2017). Feminist rhetorics and interaction design: Facilitating socially responsible design. In L. Potts & M. J. Salvo (Eds.), *Rhetoric and experience architecture* (pp. 84–110). Parlor Press.

Shah, J. J., Smith, S. M. & Vargas-Hernandez, N. (2003). Metrics for measuring ideation effectiveness. *Design Studies, 24*(2), 111–134.

Smith, G. F. (1998). Idea-generation techniques: A formulary of active ingredients. *The Journal of Creative Behavior, 32*(2), 107–133.

Stanford d.school. (2018). *Design thinking bootleg.* Hasso Plattner Institute of Design. https://dschool.stanford.edu/resources/design-thinking-bootleg.

4. Rapid Prototyping

Krys Gollihue
RED HAT, INC.

Definition and Background

An integral step in **user-centered design** and design thinking is prototyping, the process of building a model for a project so that it can be user tested and revised based on feedback. While prototypes are complete, they are not final or perfect; they are meant to test ideas, questions, or assumptions that designers have encountered through ideation or iteration. Often considered a slow exercise, prototyping takes time to complete because designers need to consider the tangible facets of their design, which may require attention to multiple options to build something and comparisons of costs vs. benefits.

Rapid prototyping is a version of prototyping where designers build a specific part of a project to be tested. Rather than taking time and resources to produce a full prototype that will have to be revised, rapid prototypes make the ideas of a project tangible enough to receive feedback in the short-term (IDEO, n.d.). The designer then returns to the process of **iterating**—revising the component based on feedback—and then **testing** another component or an added revision.

Rapid prototyping is used in developing and refining 3D models, websites, processes, user interactions, physical computing projects, and more. It can be accomplished through computer-assisted design (CAD) software, paper prototypes, play-acting scenarios, storyboards, mock-ups, etc. (IDEO, n.d.). Rather than operating as a complete, yet unrefined, product, it is a stepping stone between the ideation or brainstorming phase and the fully realized prototype (Perkins, 2015).

In technical and professional communication practices, rapid prototyping takes on these same principles of manufacturing through the process of focused and repeated drafts. Whether in content creation, user interface design, social media, or simple long-form drafts, writers and communicators can present incremental changes to stakeholders and audiences, test their efficacy, and make changes on a repeated cycle so that no single draft must be overhauled entirely. As Danielle Koupf (2017) has argued, such version control, or as they call it, "tinkering" in the writing process develops a sense of openness, "flexibility, [and] the writer's sense of the options available to him or her." Rapid prototyping makes room for the inevitable changes in audience *and* communicator's needs, desires, and investments and promotes creativity in addressing complex communication problems.

DOI: https://doi.org/10.37514/TPC-B.2022.1725.2.04

■ Design Application

While the term *rapid prototyping* was first applied in manufacturing to describe how 3D printing was used to test individual parts of a manufactured object, the concept has been extrapolated to various other communities and spaces of practice (Campbell et al., 2012). Makerspaces, for example, are collaborative workspaces that house consumer-grade technologies for ideating, prototyping, and testing designs. These spaces use rapid prototyping tools like FDM (fused deposition modeling) and SLA (stereolithography) printers, CAD software, conductive inks and threads, breadboards, sensors, and so on. Often, makerspaces will also contain lower-stakes rapid prototyping materials such as sticky notes, LEGO blocks, markers, and modeling clay that are used in the early stages of ideation and prototyping.

Because maker culture is so closely tied to start-up and design processes, which require quick production and scale, rapid prototyping in makerspaces is commonly used to develop new ideas or products through the process of prototyping, reviewing, and refining (Perkins, 2015). An example of this might be in the development of a new design for a phone case. The designer might first build a 3D model of the case using paper or modeling clay, testing whether it is the correct size. After measuring the model, they would then draft a digital 3D file of the case using CAD software and print it using cheaper filament, testing ergonomics and manufacturing times. Finally, once the designer has a good model, they may print it using different flexible materials to test which holds up the longest. This process allows the designer to isolate and test otherwise interdependent elements of a design and quickly deploy the product to its test or target market.

One of the major benefits of employing a rapid prototyping process is that it increases communication and trust between developers and their clients (Jain, 2018). By consistently testing ideas with the communities that will use, benefit from, or be impacted by the project, makers have the opportunity to build something that users will actually use, and use well, for its intended purpose.

■ Pedagogical Integration

In the technical communication classroom, rapid prototyping may be an exercise integrated with student assignments, especially those that integrate the expertise of students from across disciplines to design solutions to larger societal problems or issues on campus. Students may be assigned low- to high-fidelity prototyping projects following their proposed designed solutions. For example, students may create a wireframe for a mobile app they propose or fabricate their model via 3D printing and other CNC (computer numerically controlled) milling methods. It is important to consider the accessibility and learning curve in these prototyping tools when choosing which technology to deploy.

As an example, in one of my technical communication courses, students worked with a sustainable technology nonprofit to develop communication materials that would boost engagement on social media. Students created several series of mock-ups of a Snapchat filter to show the client and receive feedback. Each mock-up highlighted a different design element, such as text features, animation, color, content, and GPS functionality. Using different materials and software, the group was able to make individual choices about design incrementally rather than making a complete design and having to start from scratch based on feedback.

Another example can be found in Jason Tham's (2021) pedagogical experiment with prototyping in a TPC course, where students built analog and digital prototypes to demonstrate the viability of their ideas and proposed solutions. In his case study, Tham reported the affordances of materializing ideas as well as the constraints of a coursework setting for the purposes of experiencing design thinking. Nevertheless, Tham still recommended the use of prototyping as a meaningful learning activity for TPC students.

Apart from its active learning benefits, rapid prototyping may help students value the design process and not just the end product. While the prototyping may be *rapid*, it helps students slow down their design thinking by deliberating on their design intentions, tools or platform choices, and assessment criteria. Additionally, rapid prototyping provides opportunities for students to materialize, test, and iterate their design. This promotes attention to user needs and responsible designer reaction based on the early user experience of the prototype.

■ References and Recommended Readings

Campbell, I., Bourell, D. & Gibson, I. (2012). Additive manufacturing: Rapid prototyping comes of age. *Rapid Prototyping Journal*, *18*(4), 255–258. https://doi.org/10.1108/13552541211231563.

IDEO. (n.d.). *Rapid prototyping*. Design Kit. http://www.designkit.org/methods/26.

Jain, A. (2018, June 4). *A beginner's guide to rapid prototyping*. freeCodeCamp. https://www.freecodecamp.org/news/a-beginners-guide-to-rapid-prototyping–71e8722c17df/.

Koupf, D. (2017). Proliferating textual possibilities: Toward pedagogies of critical-creative tinkering. *Composition Forum*, *35*. http://compositionforum.com/issue/35/proliferating.php.

Perkins, S. (2015, December 18). *What is prototyping anyway?* UNHCR Innovation. https://www.unhcr.org/innovation/what-is-prototyping-anyway/.

Tham, J. (2021). Engaging design thinking and making in technical and professional communication pedagogy. *Technical Communication Quarterly*, *30*(4), 392–409. https://doi.org/10.1080/10572252.2020.1804619.

5. Testing

Bradley Dilger
PURDUE UNIVERSITY

▪ Definition and Background

For many technical communicators and designers, testing is the most advanced step in the design thinking process, following research, *prototyping*, and development (Pope-Ruark et al., 2019). The basic framework is simple: Ask users of a document, product, and/or system to use it, observe and guide their interaction, record how well they achieve design goals, and use that information to guide future design work. Testing, then, is one of the strongly data-driven components of design thinking, complementing user research and prototyping in empowering designers to make design decisions based on real world use. By providing direct feedback about users' engagement, testing can be the engine of *iteration* that should be at the heart of design thinking.

Testing is often strongly identified with usability testing, and particularly the *usability* of websites, given the widespread influence of Jakob Nielsen (1997, 1999), Steve Krug (2009, 2013), and Carol Barnum (2001, 2020). As Barnum (2020) observes, the ISO definition of usability is the benchmark: "The extent to which a system, product or service can be used by specified users to achieve specified goals with effectiveness, efficiency and satisfaction in a specified context of use" (p. 11). Most designers have moved away from a rigid focus on usability to broader thinking about user experience, and testing has followed suit.

The researchers noted above have popularized a streamlined "discount" approach to testing which limits the complexity and number of test sessions in order to simplify testing and hopefully make it more common. While acknowledging that larger quantitative studies are sometimes necessary or desirable, Nielsen, Krug, and Barnum explicitly (and repeatedly, and sometimes stridently) argue that expensive, laboratory-like test conditions are not necessary for designers to achieve meaningful results. "Zero users give zero insights," writes Nielsen (2000). "As soon as you collect data from a single test user, your insights shoot up and you have already learned almost a third of all there is to know about the usability of the design." For these researchers, the limitations of small-scale testing using informal methods are far exceeded by the benefits of working directly with participants to learn about a product's successes and pinch points firsthand.

While testing websites for usability often dominates conversations about testing on design and user experience websites, or even in textbooks (e.g., Markel & Selber, 2018), anything built with a design process can benefit from testing—instructions, smartphone apps, promotional materials, or election ballots (see

Rachael Sullivan's *design ethics* example, or Jarrett & Redish, 2020). Testing can measure accessibility, persuasion, error tolerance, and more, and other research methods can be integrated into the process. For example, short posttest surveys can measure how well users remember critical information. Focus groups formed from multiple testers can shape the next steps for design teams. And testing can come at any stage of the design process, engaging wireframes, prototypes, or designs released to the public. See Digital.gov for widely used resources that describe how to conduct tests and demonstrate how testing can be integrated into design processes: for example, consent forms, materials for conducting practice tests, and case studies from experienced practitioners—many once part of the now-archived Usability.gov.

◼ Design Application

In a typical test as described by Nielsen, Krug, and/or Barnum, two facilitators work with a participant in a comfortable setting, perhaps even a coffee shop or employee break room. One facilitator guides the participant through a prepared list of tasks; the other takes notes and/or operates recording equipment such as a camera (for testing paper prototypes, products, or documents) or screencasting software (for testing apps, web pages, or software). For example, the facilitator may ask a participant to envision themselves in the following scenario and complete a set of tasks:

> Sample scenario:
>
> We are testing a mobile app for a pizza restaurant. Please use the app to order two pizzas for a party. Have the pizzas delivered. Please use the address and credit card number on this note card.
>
> Tasks:
>
> 1. Start a new order and add a plain cheese pizza.
> 2. Add a second pizza with black olives on one side and green olives on the other.
> 3. Enter your address and save it as the "Home" address for future orders.

When completing the tasks, participants are often asked to use the think-aloud protocol, a technique where they explain their actions and intentions "out loud" as they go, offering a richer data stream to facilitators. Generally, test facilitators do not ask questions during the session, but might do so in a short debriefing afterward. Participants are typically offered small incentives such as a gift card. The process is repeated for a small number of participants, usually five, and then a brief report is written to share with clients and designers if they are not directly involved or present to observe the test process.

As noted above, advocates of the "discount" approach to testing emphasize the goal is not generalizable research but providing designers with data-driven guidance for iteration. For this reason, testing best practices emphasize testing with a small number of participants and focus less on identifying test participants representative of user populations. Krug (2010) suggests other forms of user research can adjust for any inaccuracies arising from "non-representative" users. Indeed, he lowers the oft-quoted number of five users per test session—established by Robert Virzi (1992) and confirmed by Nielsen (2000)—to three, arguing that increased iteration is more likely to find ways to achieve designers' goals. "Recruiting loosely," as Krug describes it (2010, p. 42), is also an opportunity to ensure designers are not excluding historically marginalized populations when identifying test participants.

■ Pedagogical Integration

Testing is a common exercise in technical communication courses (Summers & Watt, 2015), and learning to use testing for diverse purposes has many potential future uses. Direct contact with end users can help draw attention to other parts of the design process, such as *empathizing* with audiences, and the hands-on nature of testing makes it ideal for active learning. Particularly in *usability* studies or user experience research courses, students may be asked to devise methods and conduct product testing (Zhou, 2014). As with any pedagogical activities in technical communication, instructors should remind students of the critical and ethical dimensions of design. For testing, ethics is especially important, given that the sources mentioned above and testing resources commonly found using web searches focus heavily on web usability, where utility, expediency, and functionality are prioritized, sometimes carelessly.

For an introductory technical communication course, testing can be situated as a module or course unit, or can be integrated into larger projects to encourage iteration and data-driven thinking. Either way, practicing testing in class can scaffold learning by providing a ready source of test participants and opportunities for mutual assistance—students can rotate between facilitator, assistant, and participant roles, gaining perspective about the challenges of each. Available literature on remote testing (e.g., Moran & Pernice, 2020) facilitates its application in online or hybrid courses.

Though the widespread adoption of "discount" methods (Nielsen, 1997) has reduced barriers to testing, it remains labor-intensive, and technical communication instructors must allow adequate time for students to plan tests, analyze data, and draft reports. Students should seek feedback from their instructors, peers, or collaborators at each of these stages. Though testing takes a lot of work, the insights it provides are almost always worth it. Carefully planned testing not only makes better documents and products, but ensures they work for all audiences and keeps the needs of many different users in mind. Joseph Bartolotta et al.

(2018) and sources mentioned above (Summers & Watt, 2015; Zhou, 2014) offer more guidance for technical communication instructors seeking to meaningfully integrate testing into their curricula—and to continue the necessary work of broadening the focus of testing from web usability.

■ References and Recommended Readings

Barnum, C. M. (2020). *Usability testing essentials: Ready, set . . . test!* (2nd ed.). Morgan Kaufmann.

Barnum, C. M. (2001). *Usability testing and research.* Longman.

Bartolotta, J., Newmark, J. & Bourelle, T. (2018). Engaging with online design: Undergraduate user-participants and the practice-level struggles of usability learning. *Communication Design Quarterly, 5*(3), 63–72.

Jarrett, C. & Redish, G. (2020, May 4). How to test the usability of documents. *UXmatters.* https://www.uxmatters.com/mt/archives/2020/05/how-to-test-the-usability-of-documents.php.

Krug, S. (2010). *Rocket surgery made easy: The do-it-yourself guide to finding and fixing usability problems.* New Riders.

Krug, S. (2013). *Don't make me think, revisited: A common sense approach to web usability* (3rd ed.). New Riders.

Markel, M. & Selber, S. (2018). *Technical communication* (12th ed.). Bedford/St. Martin's.

Moran, K. & Pernice, K. (2020). *Remote moderated usability tests: How to do them.* Nielsen Norman Group. https://www.nngroup.com/articles/moderated-remote-usability-test/.

Nielsen, J. (1993). *Usability engineering.* Academic Press.

Nielsen, J. (1997, January 1). *Discount usability for the web.* Nielsen Norman Group. https://www.nngroup.com/articles/web-discount-usability/.

Nielsen, J. (1999). *Designing web usability.* New Riders.

Nielsen, J. (2000, March 18). *Why you only need to test with 5 users.* Nielsen Norman Group. https://www.nngroup.com/articles/why-you-only-need-to-test-with-5-users/.

Pope-Ruark, R., Moses, J. & Tham, J. (2019). Iterating the literature: An early annotated bibliography of design-thinking resources. *Journal of Business and Technical Communication, 33*(4), 456–465.

Summers, S. & Watt, A. (2015). Quick and dirty usability testing in the technical communication classroom. In *2015 IEEE International Professional Communication Conference (IPCC)* (pp. 1–4). IEEE.

Virzi, R. A. (1992). Redefining the test phase of usability evaluation: How many subjects is enough? *Human Factors, 34,* 457–468.

Zhou, Q. (2014). "That usability course": What technical communication programs get wrong about usability and how to fix it. *Communication Design Quarterly, 2*(3), 25–27.

6. Iteration

Emma J. Rose
UNIVERSITY OF WASHINGTON TACOMA

Cody Reimer
UNIVERSITY OF WISCONSIN–STOUT

Definition and Background

Iteration refers to the stage in the design thinking process of making changes to a system, whether it is a product or service, in order to make improvements. To successfully design a usable system, the design process must include three key principles: an early focus on users and tasks, empirical measurement, and iterative design (Gould & Lewis, 1985). Iteration is a key stage in the design process where new features are added and existing problems are corrected, resulting in a new version. It is a series of incremental improvements in a development lifecycle accomplished through *ideating*, modeling, *testing*, revising, and then repeating that process as necessary. As key as iteration is to the design thinking process, in TPC iteration can take many forms, especially within the drafting and writing process. Whether it is making incremental changes to an existing draft or starting from scratch, iteration is important for both writers and designers.

Design is often an interplay between *ideation* and iteration (Greever, 2015). As Jennifer Sano-Franchini demonstrated in her entry, ideation is the process of coming up with and elaborating as many new design ideas as quickly as possible, while iteration is the process of getting feedback on designs and making changes in order to improve them. Designers start with many ideas and concepts represented by low-fidelity prototypes such as sketches, which are then winnowed down over time as they are iterated and changed and move into a higher level of fidelity which moves towards the final version of a system. Bill Buxton (2007) referred to this process of moving from many ideas to one as the design funnel.

Iteration is both a process and a product. The process of iteration is embodied in the design mindset that feedback and input will improve a product. Feedback may come from peers during review or stakeholders within an organization, but most often, and ideally, it comes from representative users who are providing input via applied research methods such as *usability* testing. In terms of iteration as a product, a new version of a design or changes to design is referred to as "an iteration," which represents a snapshot of a design at a single point in time. Iterations help reduce the redundancy created by different approaches, such as parallel design, wherein different designs are built simultaneously.

DOI: https://doi.org/10.37514/TPC-B.2022.1725.2.06

■ Design Application

Working iteratively is a key mindset for designers and design thinkers. An important part of design is expecting to get feedback, input, and data that will shape and change a design. ***Prototyping*** and creating early versions of systems helps encourage iteration rather than waiting until a system is complete to share it with others. The speed of iteration is dependent on organizational context, but with the increase in popularity of approaches like agile software development and lean UX, being able to iterate rapidly is an important skill (Gothelf & Seiden, 2013). Proponents of lean UX point to rapid iteration as a means to stay competitive with cost and time (Aarlien & Colomo-Palacios, 2020). In their systematic review of literature on lean UX, David Aarlien and Ricardo Colomo-Palacios (2020) list its key principles: early validation, cross-functional design, solving user problems, measuring performance indicators, and applying tools flexibly (p. 5).

As designers iterate through models, they can evaluate the user experience of each model to aid in subsequent revisions. Low-fidelity models are cheap but abstracted, while higher fidelity comes with higher confidence in the user experience data but also a higher resource cost. According to Jakob Nielsen (2011), the recommended number of iterations for a design is at least two (meaning at least three versions), but the more the better, he suggests, though he also notes the existence of diminishing returns. The limit to the number of iterations is often time, as iterations are cheap compared to alternatives such as parallel design.

The video game industry has benefited from shrinking the time between iterations. As business models shift to longer life cycles for games, releasing new content for existing software generates significant revenue. That content must be tested within the contexts of the existing game, and the content is on a brisk release schedule. Many video game companies iterate with the speed low fidelity affords while gaining the confidence high fidelity permits. This is accomplished by:

- tracking user data and, in some cases, releasing that data back to users for them to pore over so as to better enable what in gaming argot is called "theorycrafting" (Paul, 2011),
- employing proxy servers as "test realms" where they can test code without disrupting service,
- stress-testing changes by controlling player access to those test realms, and
- supporting quantitative analysis with qualitative inquiry.

Riot Games rapidly iterates in their video game *League of Legends*, which uses a player test realm to implement, test, and adjust changes before monthly patches to the live servers. As Cody Reimer (2017) shows, Riot balances quantitative and qualitative feedback to ensure the constant and numerous changes improve user experience. They manage this by releasing typically proprietary player data to players in order to fuel discussion, and then engaging in that discussion on both official and unofficial forums.

Player-developer discussion often focuses on changes being made to the game, such as adjustments for balance or additions of new characters. Lee Sherlock (2016) discusses Riot's technical documentation, specifically patch notes, itemizing changes for each iteration of *League of Legends*. Framing a changelog genre, something often written for experts, for a player audience means communicating both technical coding changes (what was changed and how) as well as design philosophy (why it was changed in this way). Riot's patch notes exemplify one prominent way iteration appears in TPC.

■ Pedagogical Integration

When teaching design, building in opportunities for iteration is key. As is the case with many creative processes, iterative design varies in execution. Different disciplines approach it differently: Modeling (sketches, paper prototypes, wireframes, etc.), testing (usability in its myriad forms), and revising are adapted to the contexts and needs of the specific discipline, practice, or strategy employing it.

For students new to the concept of iteration, instructors may compare iteration to the writing process and how each draft and revision is an iteration with opportunities for feedback. Students might benefit from thinking of sketches like reading notes, wireframes like rough drafts, and the finished design like a polished deliverable. Another way to introduce students to iteration is to have them explore platforms such as Wikipedia, Google Docs, and GitHub, or iterative project management models like Agile and Scrum. Ask students to examine or trace how specific iterations in these models evolve over time and how feedback is key to shaping each iteration.

In order for students to experience iteration as product and process, it should be built into the structure of the course. Make each iteration a discrete stage and build assignments around each deliverable. Take, for example, a project where teams of students are designing a website for a community partner. Build in three iterations: early sketches, prototype, and a functional site. At each iteration, students should engage in rounds of critique and, if possible, usability testing, to further explore how the design is refined over time and how each level of fidelity is an opportunity to explore and improve design elements based on feedback and data. Using community- or client-based projects is a valuable way to teach iteration since each design iteration can be shared with stakeholders for review and critique. Early client concerns can be addressed in early, low-fidelity iterations before too much time has been spent. Further, the choice of fidelity can highlight the rhetorical nature of iterative design (Rose & Tenenberg, 2017) as different stakeholders might not understand or appreciate lower fidelity "unfinished" work.

Critique and revision are key components of iteration. Students should have the opportunity to engage in daily or weekly design critiques or reviews. One helpful mindset to teach to students is to embrace feedback with patience and view critiques as opportunities to improve their design. It can also be helpful to generate a set of questions that is used consistently in regular reviews, such as: "What have we done so far?" "What works in the current design?" "What still needs to be done and how might we do that?" Keeping a constant approach to reviewing design can reduce redundancy and create common expectations that can aid in the iteration process.

■ References and Recommended Readings

Aarlien, D. & Colomo-Palacios, R. (2020, July). Lean UX: A systematic literature review. In *International Conference on Computational Science and Its Applications* (pp. 500–510). Springer, Cham.

Buxton, B. (2007). *Sketching user experiences: Getting the design right and the right design.* Morgan Kaufmann.

Da Silva, T. S., Martin, A., Maurer, F. & Silveira, M. (2011, August). User-centered design and agile methods: A systematic review. In *2011 AGILE Conference* (pp. 77–86). IEEE.

Gothelf, J. & Seiden, J. (2013). *Lean UX: Applying Lean principles to improve user experience.* O'Reilly Media.

Gould, J. D. & Lewis, C. (1985, March). Designing for usability: Key principles and what designers think. *Communications of the ACM, 28*(3), 300–311.

Greever, T. (2015). *Articulating design decisions: Communicate with stakeholders, keep your sanity, and deliver the best user experience.* O'Reilly Media.

Karat, J. & Karat, C. M. (2003). The evolution of user-centered focus in the human-computer interaction field. *IBM Systems Journal, 42*(4), 532–541.

Lepore, T. (2010, May). Sketches and wireframes and prototypes! Oh my! Creating your own magical wizard experience. *UXmatters.* https://www.uxmatters.com/mt/archives/2010/05/sketches-and-wireframes-and-prototypes-oh-my-creating-your-own-magical-wizard-experience.php.

Nielsen, J. (2011, January). *Parallel & iterative design + competitive testing = high usability.* Nielsen Norman Group. https://www.nngroup.com/articles/parallel-and-iterative-design/.

Paul, C. A. (2011). Optimizing play: How theorycrafting changes gameplay & design. *Game Studies, 11*(2). http://gamestudies.org/1102/articles/paul.

Reimer, C. (2017). Dialogic, data-driven design: UX and League of Legends. In L. Potts & M. Salvo (Eds.), *Rhetoric and experience architecture* (pp. 241–257). Parlor Press.

Rose, E. & Tenenberg, J. (2017). Making practice-level struggles visible: Researching UX practice to inform pedagogy. *Communication Design Quarterly, 5*(1), 89–97.

Sherlock, L. (2016). Patching as design rhetoric: Tracing the framing and delivery of iterative content documentation in online games. In J. deWinter & R. M. Moeller (Eds.), *Computer games and technical communication* (pp. 157–170). Routledge.

Spinuzzi, C. (2005). The methodology of participatory design. *Technical Communication, 52*(2), 163–174.

Sullivan, P. (1989). Beyond a narrow conception of usability testing. *IEEE Transactions on Professional Communication, 32*(4), 254–264.

Taylor, T. L. (2006). Beyond management: Considering participatory design and governance in player culture. *First Monday.* http://firstmonday.org/ojs/index.php/fm/article/view/1611/1526.

Part 2: Concepts and Applications

7. Affordances

Devon Cook
PENN STATE NEW KENSINGTON

Definition and Background

Technical communicators and designers are attuned to the qualities of media and technology that support communication. Adopted from the field of psychology, the notion of affordance is used frequently in design and human-technology interaction and commonly refers to "advantageous possibilities for use" when speaking about objects and technologies. James J. Gibson (1977), who coined the term, described affordances as qualities of an environment that "offer," "provide," or "furnish" outcomes for an individual. In other words, affordances are the real or perceived qualities of things that make them useful. For example, a standard No. 2 pencil affords writing because its graphite core leaves marks when rubbed on paper. It also affords being gripped in the left or right hand because of its appropriate size and long, skinny shape. It affords erasing mistakes because of the eraser attached to one end. These affordances are obvious to most No. 2 pencil users, but the pencil has less obvious affordances as well. For instance, it also affords writing with the foot, as it can be gripped between the toes.

Design thinkers and practitioners leverage the notion of affordance to create solutions that correspond with user needs and expectations, based on the users' present and past experiences and abilities. Effective use of affordance can promote optimal *usability*—users will mentally map the possible actions in a designed object (what it *can do*) using their existing mental model informed by prior experiences (what the object *should do*). A clear match between the expected affordance and actual feature of an object would result in good user experience.

One of the major scholarly debates surrounding affordances has centered around whether or not affordances are real, material qualities of objects and environments, or instead perceptions an individual has about objects and environments. Don Norman (1999) describes "perceived affordance" as a quality of usefulness recognized by a user regardless of whether or not the affordance actually exists. Norman's example is a user believing they can use a touchscreen when the screen in question doesn't have touchscreen capabilities. Perceived affordances are an essential factor in any situation where an object, tool, or technology is being designed for use because if a user cannot correctly identify the affordances of the thing they are using, then the design is likely to fail, even if it technically works. For instance, if a user has never seen or used an eraser before, the erasing affordance of the No. 2 pencil won't matter very much.

DOI: https://doi.org/10.37514/TPC-B.2022.1725.2.07

■ Design Application

While it might be tempting to say that the perception of affordances is the only thing that matters, Ian Hutchby (2001) argues it is important to recognize that perceived affordances are still based on real, material qualities. Through experience, these real affordances influence what users will recognize in the future about the things they use and their subsequent usability. Once someone has used a pencil eraser's physical properties to erase pencil markings, they may recognize a similar affordance in a standalone eraser, even if they have never used one before. In this way, affordances can be seen as real qualities of objects or environments and not only perceived by individuals.

For technical communicators and designers of user interfaces, this means paying attention to the implicit and explicit material qualities of their design in order to optimize the benefits of certain affordances as well as **constraints**. Strategic use of affordances can prompt appropriate user behavior and lead to positive user experience. For example, lines, as a graphic element, can afford categorization of content on a page (by creating sections) as well as a visual cue that guides the eyes and facilitates reading. When applied aptly, this simple element can invoke good usability and positive user experience (see Figure 7.1).

Additionally, being cognizant of affordances can help designers and communicators identify constraints or limitations of their design and thus increase empathy for users.

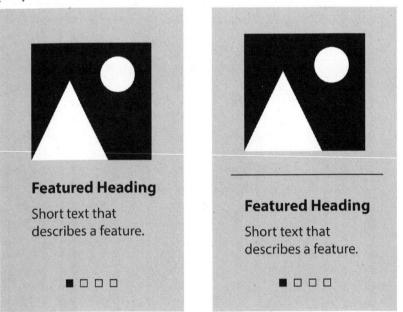

Figure 7.1. A sample use of lines in interface design to afford categorization. Image created by Tham, adapted from UX Movement, 2016, https://tinyurl.com/54yuzpwd.

Pedagogical Integration

Understanding of affordances can lead to more thoughtful and effective practices. Instructors who teach design rhetorically can adopt this understanding to promote students' attentiveness to qualities of media and technology that facilitate use and implication. A pedagogical exercise may be assessing the affordances of a conventional office chair. Students assigned to examine the design of the chair from the affordance perspective might find multiple uses beyond the traditional purpose (i.e., sitting), due to the shape, weight, and other material features that the chair offers (e.g., a sturdy chair may also be used as a step-up tool). Using a physical object in this pedagogical exercise, instead of a complex web interface, can help students focus on understanding the concept of affordances.

For a larger project, students may perform a design analysis of a website or mobile application with an eye toward specific interface design elements (e.g., lines, alignment, colors, typography, contrast, repetition, icons, etc.) to explicate the affordances of the selected elements. After the analysis, students may conduct secondary research on the historical and social forces that influence the use of the specific elements in digital design. Finally, students can make recommendations for design improvements based on their findings in the first and second part of the project.

References and Recommended Readings

Gibson, J. J. (1977). The theory of affordances. In R. Shaw & J. Bransford (Eds.), *Perceiving, acting, and knowing: Toward an ecological psychology* (pp. 67–82). Erlbaum.

Hartson, R. (2003). Cognitive, physical, sensory, and functional affordances in interaction design. *Behaviour & Information Technology, 22*(5), 315–338. https://doi.org/10.1080/01449290310001592587.

Hutchby, I. (2001). Technologies, texts and affordances. *Sociology, 35*(2), 441–456. https://doi.org/10.1177/S0038038501000219.

Maier, J. & Fadel, G. (2009). Affordance based design: A relational theory for design. *Research in Engineering Design, 20*(1), 13–27.

Nagy, P. & Neff, G. (2015). Imagined affordance: Reconstructing a keyword for communication theory. *Social Media + Society, 1*(2), 1–9.

Norman, D. A. (1999). Affordance, conventions, and design. *Interactions, 6*(3), 38–43. https://doi.org/10.1145/301153.301168.

Oliver, M. (2005). The problem with affordance. *E-Learning and Digital Media, 2*(4), 402–413.

Turner, P. (2005). Affordance as context. *Interacting with Computers, 17*(6), 787–800.

You, H. & Chen, K. (2007). Applications of affordance and semantics in product design. *Design Studies, 28*(1), 23–38.

8. Collaboration

Matthew A. Vetter
INDIANA UNIVERSITY OF PENNSYLVANIA

Definition and Background

Collaboration, to co-make or co-labor, refers to both the act and process of distributed design in technical communication, typically between two or more human actors, entities, or organizations, in response to an exigence or problem. While definitions and perspectives vary across professional and academic fields, collaboration may refer to the process of distributed meaning making and problem-solving, as well as the act of creating or designing a shared object, text, new understanding, event, or even relationship. As a method of distributed cooperation, collaboration may also include non-human agents such as computer programs, objects, environments, genres, and tools. At the intersection of design thinking and technical communication, collaboration can be understood as both an outcome of and method for design thinking processes. Because design thinking offers a framework for meta-disciplinary and meta-professional teamwork, collaborative design thinking "allows multi-professional teams to develop a mutual understanding due to its strong emphasis on team-based learning regarding both the problem and its potential solutions" (Lindberg et al., 2010). While there is a history of collaboration as discussed and practiced in pedagogical contexts (Ede & Lunsford, 1990; Holt, 2018), technical communication research has largely focused on collaboration as a practice of professional industry (Burnett & Duin, 1993; Reither & Vipond, 1989).

In design thinking, effective collaboration is (implicitly or explicitly) structured by roles, strategies, and processes. Well-defined and understood roles taken up by participants in a collaborative project aid in making explicit the expectations of collaboration. Roles may vary depending on the nature of the project and may shift within a project. In designing a collaborative multimodal project, for instance, collaborators may agree upon initial roles related to research, drafting, documentation, visual arrangement, and organization, and then shift or exchange those roles at a later point in the process. In *usability* research and *user-centered design* processes, collaboration manifests in researcher-user interactions, such as *participatory design*. Strategies for effective collaboration may include:

1. agreeing upon clear expectations and goals;
2. identifying individual roles and responsibilities;
3. establishing shared values;
4. identifying the chronological and/or geographical parameters for work expectations, such as timetables or regularly scheduled meetings;

DOI: https://doi.org/10.37514/TPC-B.2022.1725.2.08

5. utilizing generative methods of feedback for members;

6. promoting standardization for the product or outcome; and

7. agreeing upon any necessary protocols related to the production and execution of policy, governance, and resolution of conflict.

■ Design Application

Digital communication tools have expanded opportunities for all types of collaboration. One of the most well-known collaborative projects is the online encyclopedia Wikipedia. As a case study of productive collaboration, Wikipedia is a representative case study because it has enabled and defined clear roles, structures, values, and expectations for contributors. The community has also put into place clear methods for feedback and communication between members and formulated clear guidelines and policies for resolving conflicts and creating policy regarding content and content creation. Wikipedia accomplishes much of this collaboration because it has enabled a new form of economic production, what is known as commons-based peer production (CBPP). In CBPP, collaborators work within a loose system of other editors (as well as non-human agents such as bots, policies, and the wiki platform) separated by both chronological and geographical distance. Despite this lack of organization around geographic and chronological parameters, the crowd-sourced model is successful because it enables self-involved motivation of multiple contributors over a long period of time (Benkler, 2002). Professional technical communicators, designers, and students should look to contemporary successful examples in order to understand the collaborative strategies and processes.

■ Pedagogical Integration

Processes of collaboration are extremely context dependent. Mike Sharples et al. (1993) identify three unique processes in collaborative writing projects: sequential, parallel, and reciprocal. In a sequential writing process, collaborators take turns contributing to a text before passing it to the next individual. This process allows writers to build on a work-in-progress and lends coherence to the text. In a parallel writing process, collaborators work on different sections simultaneously. Such a process takes less time but may require more editorial work to achieve coherence when the sections are combined. In the third process identified by Sharples et al., reciprocal writing, collaborators simultaneously work on a textual product through discussion, drafting, and revision. Depending on the level of experience of the collaborators, this process may be better suited to initial brainstorming and outlining.

Since design thinking advocates for collaborative problem-solving, students may be assigned team projects to exercise collaborative design and decision making (Wolfe, 2010). The scale of collaboration could range from paired students to large class groups. When designing and deploying collaborative learning projects, instructors should identify the specific exigency (or motivation) for student collaboration and provide scaffolding to the collaboration process, such as Sharples et al.'s guidelines. Students should also be introduced to tools and technologies that can support their collaboration. Matt Barton and Karl Klint (2011) have demonstrated that digital platforms like Google Docs can be a viable shared space for student collaborations.

■ References and Recommended Readings

Barton, M. & Klint, K. (2011). A student's guide to collaborative writing technologies. In C. Lowe & P. Zemliansky (Eds.), *Writing spaces: Readings on writing, Vol. 1* (pp. 319–332). Parlor Press. https://wac.colostate.edu/books/writingspaces2/barton-and -klint--a-students-guide.pdf.

Benkler, Y. (2002). Coase's penguin, or, Linux and the nature of the firm. *Yale Law Journal, 112*(3), 367–445.

Burnett, R. E. & Duin, A. H. (1993). Collaboration in technical communication: A research continuum. *Technical Communication Quarterly, 2*(1), 5–21.

Ede, L. & Lunsford, A. (1990). *Singular texts/plural authors: Perspectives on collaborative writing*. Southern Illinois University Press.

Holt, M. (2018). *Collaborative learning as democratic practice: A history*. National Council of Teachers of English.

Lindberg, T., Noweski, C. & Meinel, C. (2010). Evolving discourses on design thinking: How design cognition inspires meta-disciplinary creative collaboration. *Technoetic Arts: A Journal of Speculative Research, 8*(1), 31–37. https://doi.org/10.1386/tear.8.1.31/1.

Reither, J. & Vipond, D. (1989). Writing as collaboration. *College English, 51*(8), 855–867. https://doi.org/10.2307/378091.

Sharples, M., Goodlet, J. S., Beck, E. E., Wood, C. C., Easterbrook, S. M. & Plowman, L. (1993). Research issues in the study of computer supported collaborative writing. In M. Sharples (Ed.), *Computer supported collaborative writing* (pp. 9–28). Springer.

Wolfe, J. (2010). *Team writing: A guide to working in groups*. Bedford/St. Martin's.

9. Constraints

Jeff Naftzinger
SACRED HEART UNIVERSITY

Definition and Background

Constraints are factors in a situation—related to the technologies, users, and contexts that are being designed for—that help to limit and direct the choices designers make in anticipation of their product's use case. A wide range of factors can function as constraints: Some are technical, some are related to the users, and some are related to the contexts being designed for. The technical or technological constraints are a facet of a technology that "confines [a designer's] ability to achieve [a] desired outcome" (Mettler & Wulf, 2019, p. 249) or a user's ability to interact with that design to achieve the desired outcome. The intended users of a product, and their understandings, abilities, and the situations they will be in, can shape how the designers balance their wants and intentions with the wants/needs of the users and the ways users might interact with the product. The rules, standards, and expectations of the document or design can shape what the designers are able to do and what the users are looking for with that product (see Herijgers & Maat, 2017). All of these constraints should be taken into account as designers make choices about their product and revise it through the design process.

Constraints help designers determine what the technologies and situations they're working in allow, what they require, what they discourage, and what they refuse (Davis & Chouinard, 2017, p. 2), and these constraints help designers make choices that direct users towards an intended use or outcome—or away from unintended ones. Perhaps because of synonyms like "limitations" and "confines," constraints are sometimes seen as a negative aspect of a technology or situation, but thinking about constraints helps designers determine how the product fits within the contexts it is created for, how it fits with the ways users might interact with the product, and how those interactions fit with the designers' intended outcomes (Gabriel-Petit, 2016).

Design Application

One illustration of technological constraints is the limitations set by Twitter for tweets: They are limited to 280 characters; (up to) four images, one video, or a poll; and they can link to pages outside of twitter. With these constraints in mind, writers know exactly what their text can contain. The technological constraints of tweets can also help the writers imagine how their audience will interact with the text, because they know a tweet can really only be ignored, read, liked, retweeted,

DOI: https://doi.org/10.37514/TPC-B.2022.1725.2.09

or replied to with similar constraints as above. Knowing how users can interact with a text because of these constraints can enable writers to engineer interactions (like encouraging retweets or responses) or limit others (like locking replies). If these constraints fit the use case, then writers can imagine how to design an effective text; if they don't, then writers can begin to select a new medium and work on identifying its constraints.

The use of situational constraints in design can be seen in the concept of "unpleasant design," in which designers implement "processes and tools . . . aimed specifically at making people uncomfortable or interfering with their use of public space" (Savicic & Savic, 2014, p. 3). Unpleasant designs demonstrate how designers can be given constraints that shape their designs, which in turn result in providing constraints that shape how users interact with the design. A standard park bench, for example, allows multiple people to sit down on it or one single person to lay down on it. If designers have been given a situational constraint like encouraging sitting while discouraging sleeping, then they must devise ways to implement constraints that push users towards that intended outcome, like inserting an armrest in the middle of the bench. The situational constraint shapes the design, and the design shapes the interactions: Potential visitors can still sit on the bench, but the arm rest prevents them from laying down on it.

While *affordances* can help designers think about what is offered or encouraged, constraints can help designers determine how to narrow their possibilities and balance what they *want* to do with what they *can*, or *should*, do in a given situation. Thinking about constraints can aid in the processes of *ideation*, by narrowing the choices that are available, and in *iteration*, by highlighting new constraints that need to influence the next design. Thinking about constraints helps designers see how their goals can, or must, be reconciled with the perceived technological and situational limitations they're designing for, and they are one aspect of *critical making* and design thinking.

▪ Pedagogical Integration

To better understand how constraints shape their design choices, students can work both analytically, to identify the constraints that shaped existing documents/designs, or productively, to identify constraints as they create new documents/designs.

To identify the constraints that led to a design, students can be given an existing product and tasked with identifying both how the technologies, users, and contexts shaped it and how the design shapes the ways users interact with it. For example, students can take a tweet from an organization and identify how the constraints have resulted in choices around the verbal and visual elements that were included, or even the medium itself, and they can determine how these technological constraints shape the ways users are able to—or encouraged to—interact with the tweet. Or they can be shown an example of unpleasant design—like a park bench—and determine the technological constraints that are encouraging and discouraging certain behaviors and what situational constraints may have led to those design choices (like public policies and community standards). After analyzing the constraints that led to a document/design, students can also be asked to make a new iteration of the product that more effectively responds to the constraints of the situation or implements new constraints that result in different user interactions.

To identify and use constraints productively, students can be given a scenario and work to identify the constraints that would lead to an effective design for the situation and users. For example, they might be asked to take on the role of an organization announcing a new product or event, and they can be given constraints like a specific audience and a specific interaction or outcome for that audience. Students can then identify the situational constraints of that audience and outcome, and determine a medium that would be most effective; with the medium in mind, they identify the technological constraints that would affect their text and the technological constraints they can use to encourage their desired outcome. They can also be given new constraints to determine how their design would need to change in order to respond effectively. By negotiating changing aspects of the situation or intended users, students can better understand how the constraints work towards narrowing, directing, and changing their decisions.

■ References and Recommended Readings

Davis, J. L. & Chouinard, J. B. (2017). Theorizing affordances: From request to refuse. *Bulletin of Science, Technology & Society, 36*(4), 241–248. https://doi.org/10.1177/02704 67617714944.

Gabriel-Petit, P. (2016, May 31). The role of constraints in design innovation. *UXmatters.* https://www.uxmatters.com/mt/archives/2016/05/the-role-of-constraints-in-design -innovation.php.

Herijgers, M. & Maat, H. P. (2017). Navigating contextual constraints in discourse: Design explications in institutional talk. *Discourse Studies, 19*(3), 272–290. https://doi .org/10.1177/1461445617701811.

Kress, G. (2009). *Multimodality: A social semiotic approach to contemporary communication.* Routledge.

Mettler, T. & Wulf, J. (2019). Physiolytics at the workplace: Affordances and constraints of wearables use from an employee's perspective. *Information Systems Journal, 29*(1), 245–273.

Norman, D. (2013). *The design of everyday things* (Revised and expanded edition). Basic Books.

Savicic, G. & Savic, S. (2014). Unpleasant design. Designing out unwanted behaviour. In *Proceedings of the 5th STS Italia Conference: A Matter of Design. Making Society Through Science and Technology* (pp. 975–988). https://infoscience.epfl.ch/record/207789.

10. Contextual Inquiry

Thomas M. Geary
TIDEWATER COMMUNITY COLLEGE

■ Definition and Background

An integral methodology in the initial empathize phase of the d.school's design thinking process, contextual inquiry, a structured shadowing and analysis of stakeholders in their environment, attempts to understand the behaviors, actions, and inner workings of an organization or workplace. Probing and analytical, contextual inquiry assists designers in knowing how a culture operates, how products are used, and how decisions are made (Beckman & Barry, 2007). Designers experience a user's vocabulary, habits, and workflow, asking for clarification and explanation of tasks and processes with the goal of learning more about the wicked problems faced. User-centricity with awareness of context meets the needs of today's workforce and results in the development of stronger services and ideas. Sara L. Beckman and Michael Barry (2007) write, "Today, marketing organizations must do more than appeal to an undifferentiated mass market. They must learn to deliver to individual customers. Doing so requires that they better understand the context in which those customers live" (p. 31).

Of the various field research methodologies that are employed in the design process to interact with target users, contextual inquiry is perhaps the most involved. Created in 1988 by Hugh R. Beyer and Karen Holtzblatt, contextual inquiry is a systematic approach that contrasts with—and may be used in conjunction with—other forms of information gathering such as focus groups, research, diaries, ethnographic interviews, and informal observations. In this structured ethnographic framework, a user's experiences and actions are captured in the moment rather than recalled later. The three key components are working in context, establishing a partnership, and maintaining focus through clarification of concerns (Raven & Flanders, 1996). At the core of contextual inquiry is observation intended to identify silos and communication breakdowns and uncover tacit knowledge in a unique environment. Holtzblatt and Beyer (2017) analogize this inquiry process to an apprentice and master: The designer learns from the customer to explore how systems work. They promote intense analysis by the apprentice to gain knowledge from the master: "Probe emotional energy to find its origin and motivations" (Holtzblatt & Beyer, 2017, p. 55). Verbal and nonverbal forms of communication, including body language and gestures, are observed. The intensive, in-depth interview process provides designers with a strong grasp of workplace successes and obstacles.

DOI: https://doi.org/10.37514/TPC-B.2022.1725.2.10

Design Application

Best suited for complex processes and experts in their field, the extensive process of contextual inquiry includes a series of observations conducted with the goal of capturing user needs, product potential, and environmental barriers—both visible and invisible. Prepared with a research brief of the target audience, the facilitator begins the contextual inquiry with preliminary discussion of expectations followed by an active observation in which the user is encouraged to focus on their everyday experiences (Beyer & Holtzblatt, 1995). Demonstrations of their typical workplace interactions with a product, rather than only explanations, are solicited as the facilitator seeks to understand the "how's" and "why's" of the user's choices. The facilitator identifies the simple tasks that an employee might overlook due to the habitual nature of the tasks (Lazar et al., 2010). Kim Salazar (2020) details a contextual inquiry experience in redesigning automobile insurance policy software for data entry. The observed specialists failed to mention several important steps of their daily tasks in interviews but were witnessed during contextual inquiry habitually cross-referencing materials and saving data despite the presence of auto-save. Through observations, the designers uncovered employee trust issues that could be addressed in new software development. These active observations are lengthy, natural, and conversational, with a focus on asking clarifying questions to acquire robust, jargon-free descriptions of tasks being performed while steering participants away from complaints or off-topic discussion.

As the designer engages in discovery via questioning in the real workplace, they build rapport through dialogue and practice empathy, an immersion into the lives of users to understand how they feel about the experience. The contextual inquiry process necessitates well-structured roles of observers and participants to achieve effective collaboration, as Matthew Vetter writes in this collection. Observers should be careful to avoid biases or assumptions and be open to new understandings. Mary Elizabeth Raven and Alicia Flanders (1996) share a story of entering a truck manufacturing site with the expectation of employees using a database in a professional setting, yet they found themselves "standing next to two men in an open assembly bay, with no air conditioning in 100-degree heat, wearing a hard hat, watching men converse in Portuguese while they pointed at the screen with grease-stained fingers" (p. 2). Interviewers should maintain ample documentation via detailed notes and even recordings. Though videotaped and virtual inquiries have become more common, Holtzblatt and Beyer (2017) note that physical presence is ideal. Post-inquiry steps include consolidation of observations and notes, qualitative coding "interpretation" sessions, and analysis and diagramming of interviews to understand patterns and trends (Beyer & Holtzblatt, 1998).

Contextual inquiry is utilized as a methodology for a wide range of industries and purposes, including the reduction of design error in surgical instruments (Moustafa et al., 2020), integration of educational technology in higher education

(Phipps & Lanclos, 2019), adoption of automatic teller machines by financial institutions (De Angeli et al., 2004), and analysis of Twitter as a platform for work engagement (Wani et al., 2017). The data and authentic behaviors revealed in the inquiry process can be beneficial to designers and businesses. Though in-depth research of users in their context often results in a strong designer-customer relationship, Michael Blechner et al. (2003) express concerns regarding the labor-intensive process in their case study of problem-based learning for medical students. They reflect that contextual inquiry, though highly structured and promising for the medical field, is time consuming, difficult in work environments that cannot excuse workers for lengthy observations or interviews, and problematic for the privacy of patient information.

Pedagogical Integration

A viable pedagogical application of contextual inquiry is to let students immerse themselves in an *in-situ* data collection and analysis exercise where they shadow a "day in the life" of select professionals in particular lines of work (preferably to the students' own interest) and journal observed practices and unique situations. Students may interview their shadowing subject, document and—with permission—record specific occurrences in the professional setting, pay attention to the ecology of work in the select environment, and interpret what their findings reveal about the employees performing their duties. Through this experiential learning exercise, students should gain direct insights into the particular professional life of their observed subjects and understand organizational culture and situational factors that contribute to the joys and struggles of specific stakeholders under study.

Keep in mind that this exercise only allows students to gain a snapshot of the particular situation and the users they observed. Upon completing the contextual inquiry, should the students elect to further investigate the user experience of the selected setting, they should read their journal and other field notes closely to identify areas for improvement that could be brought about by designed solutions. Contextual inquiry is only the beginning of ***user-centered design***.

References and Recommended Readings

Beckman, S. & Barry, M. (2007). Innovation as a learning process: Embedded design thinking. *California Review Management, 50*(1), 25–56.

Beyer, H. & Holtzblatt, K. (1995). Apprenticing with the customer. *Communications of the ACM, 38*(5), 45–52.

Beyer, H. & Holtzblatt, K. (1998). *Contextual design: Defining customer-centered systems.* Morgan Kaufmann.

Blechner, M., Monaco, V., Knox, I. & Crowley, R. (2003). Using contextual design to identify potential innovations for problem based learning. In *AMIA Annual Symposium Proceedings Archive* (pp. 91–95).

De Angeli, A., Athavankar, U., Joshi, A., Coventry, L. & Johnson, G. I. (2004). Introducing ATMs in India: A contextual inquiry. *Interacting with Computers, 16*(1), 29–44.

Holtzblatt, K. & Beyer, H. (2017). *Contextual design: Design for life* (2nd ed.). Morgan Kaufmann.

Lazar, J., Feng, J. H. & Hochheiser, H. (2010). *Research methods in human-computer interaction.* Wiley.

Moustafa, A.W., Mousa, H. & Selim, M. I. (2020). Using contextual inquiry in surgical instruments design. *International Design Journal, 10*(2), 33–38.

Norman, D. A. (2002). *The design of everyday things.* Basic Books.

Phipps, L. & Lanclos, D. (2019). Trust, innovation and risk: A contextual inquiry into teaching practices and the implications for the use of technology. *Irish Journal of Technology Enhanced Learning, 4*(1), 68–85.

Raven, M. E. & Flanders, A. (1996). Using contextual inquiry to learn about your audiences. *The Journal of Computer Documentation, 20*(1), 1–13.

Rosenfeld Halverson, E. & Sheridan, K. (2014). The maker movement in education. *Harvard Educational Review, 84*(4), 495–504.

Salazar, K. (2020, December 6). *Contextual inquiry: Inspire design by observing and interviewing users in their context.* Nielsen Norman Group. https://www.nngroup.com /articles/contextual-inquiry/.

Wani, N., Bhutkar, G. & Ekal, S. (2017). Conducting contextual inquiry of Twitter for work engagement: An Indian perspective. *International Journal of Computer Applications, 168*(9), 27–36.

11. Creativity

Emily Wierszewski
Seton Hill University

Definition and Background

Creativity is the process of assessing a problem and, in response, developing multiple innovative solutions; additionally, creativity often requires the flexibility to adapt or even discard some of those solutions in the face of *failure*. While creativity was once thought to be an innate skill, today we accept that creativity can be learned through observation, connection, and persistence (e.g., Csikszentmihalyi, 2013; Kaufman & Gregoire, 2015; Kelley & Kelley, 2013; Robinson, 2017; and Seelig, 2012). As Stefanio Zenios, co-director of the Center for Entrepreneurial Studies at Stanford, has said, because it is "a structured, systematic way to solve problems," anyone can learn to practice creativity (qtd. in Fyffe & Lee, 2016).

The creative process begins when we either observe or are given a problem. David Kelley and Tom Kelley (2013) of the IDEO global design company share stories of innovators inspired by observation. In one narrative, they describe how a medical engineer redesigned a pediatric MRI machine from a child's perspective, transforming it into a pirate ship adventure after witnessing anxious pediatric MRI patients (pp. 15–16). Creativity researchers of all stripes agree that to exercise creativity, we must be curious about and pay careful attention to our world. Because design thinking is *user-centered* and focused on *human factors*, designers need to pay special attention to the people who inhabit the world in their observations. Zenios recommends spending time studying and conversing with users, especially around moments of "challenge" in order to learn more about the problems that users face (qtd. in Fyffe & Lee, 2016). Mark A. Runco (2003) also emphasizes that creativity involves both "problem-solving and problem finding" through observation and awareness of the world (pp. 658–659).

The next stage in the creative process involves *ideation*. Creative solutions are often formed when we make novel connections between objects or ideas, thinking beyond what's obvious to discover new and meaningful relationships (Andreason, 2014; Kaufman & Gregoire, 2015; Seelig, 2012). This stage in the creative process is similar to critical thinking, in that it requires us to analyze our design problem from many angles. However, while the endgame of critical thinking is to evaluate a problem, the endgame of creativity is to develop solutions to a problem. In his 2005 commencement speech to Stanford students, Steve Jobs reflected that "Creativity is just connecting things." Jobs was known for telling the story of how an undergraduate typography course inspired the

DOI: https://doi.org/10.37514/TPC-B.2022.1725.2.11

aesthetic of the Apple computer. He was among the first to consider the relationship between visual design and computing. As was the case with Jobs' ideas for the design of the Apple computer, successful connections are often transformative and change how we think about or interact with the world (Csikszentmihalyi, 2013). In art and in poetry, these relationships are quite common and are often labeled metaphors. As the poet Jane Hirschfield put it, "The balancing between expected and unforeseen, both in aesthetic and cognitive structures, is near the center of every work of art."

Creative solutions are often the result of divergent thinking, which, as the name implies, involves the production of many original ideas that can diverge "in any direction" (Acar & Runco, 2019, p. 157). Selcuk Acar and Mark A. Runco (2019) emphasize that because divergent thinking goes in several directions, it can even involve "thinking with opposites or even contradictions" (p. 153). Creative solutions are not only wide in scope but large in number. As Eden Hennessey and Julie Mueller (2020) confirm, divergent thinking involves developing a vast number of solutions in response to a problem (p. 509). These solutions are often generated in generous quantities because divergent thinking doesn't initially require us to address the "fit" or feasibility of those solutions. In this way, divergent thinking stands in contrast to convergent thinking, "which seeks to narrow the number of alternatives based upon certain criteria, such as effectiveness, efficiency, appropriateness, usefulness, or fit" and comes later in the design process as prototypes are developed and user tested (Stuhlfaut & Windels, 2015, p. 244).

Developing a large quantity of new or unexpected ideas is a practice that is best done collaboratively. As Zenios notes, collaborating allows creators to play on one another's strengths, as well as their previous experiences and unique perspectives. "By combining those ingredients together," Zenios argues, "you can come up with new and creative ways to solve a problem" (qtd. in Fyffe & Lee, 2016). The importance of collaboration at this stage in the creative process is stressed by scholars writing about creativity in a variety of professional and educational contexts (consult, for instance, Hokanson, 2006; Hsiao et al., 2017; Lee et al., 2019; Zhong & Fan, 2016; Zidulka & Kajzer, 2018).

Finally, the influence on creativity of our environment, identities, and previous experiences as human beings cannot be overlooked. For instance, our ability to engage in creativity can be encouraged or restricted by the parameters and tone of our environment. Petro Poutanen (2013) provides an example, writing that "A normative environment that permits people to disagree may liberate people to be more creative by allowing otherwise banned discourses to emerge and stimulating additional ideas through competing views" (p. 113). This applies both to workplace and classroom settings. Scholars like Marc Santos and Megan McIntyre (2016) have written about the importance of balancing uncertainty and unknowns with appropriate support structures for students when teaching the creative process.

■ Design Application

When thinking creatively, not all of our observations and ideas will be successful. Thus, creativity necessitates a willingness to persevere through and in spite of failure. In her decades of creativity research, Nancy C. Andreason (2014) discovered that "Creative people tend to be very persistent, even when confronted with skepticism or rejection." Creativity demands not only an openness to making mistakes, but the self-awareness to learn from them (Kelley & Kelley, 2013). Although schooling and society at large have arguably conditioned most of us to fear failure, it is an expected and important part of the creative process.

Creativity manifests in both abstract and concrete forms in the design process. When conceptualizing and defining the problem space for a specific task, communicators and designers can demonstrate creativity by offering unconventional perspectives to the definition and ideation processes of design thinking. Similarly, they may be expected to articulate and realize radical solutions and ways of actualizing proposed designs through the prototyping and testing phases. Creativity is a constant strength as well as strain that sustains the design process. For technical communicators who work with design teams, it is important to understand creativity as an ongoing tide rather than a distinctive moment of inspiration. Creativity requires vigor and endurance on the part of the designer throughout the design process to ensure the materialization of exceptional solutions.

■ Pedagogical Integration

Creative thinkers are exceptional observers. Pulitzer Prize winning poet Mary Oliver (2003) concludes her poem "Yes! No!" with the following line: "To pay attention, this is our endless / and proper work." Oliver regarded attention as key to the creative process, and she wasn't alone in this thinking—the concept of mindfulness appears throughout modern creativity research. Students need to be taught observational skills and mindfulness about the world around them. Here are some ways that can be accomplished:

- Encourage students to spend time in locations related to their domains of study and to keep observational journals about what they notice people doing and how they interact with design in their environments.
- Require students to record observations related to the design problems they face, including how users interact with designs (much like the medical engineer described above in the work of Kelley & Kelley, 2013). They can learn to talk to users about their experiences.

Creative designers are proficient at making novel connections, but many students find this to be a complex, unfamiliar skill. The more practice students have with this kind of cognitive work, the more creative their design solutions will be. Below are some specific ideas for developing divergent thinking in the classroom.

- Teach students the concept of metaphor to show them a familiar, accessible way to see how unlike things can have working relationships. Show them an example of metaphor in advertisements. (If you're looking for inspiration, try car ads! A recent Mitsubishi print ad compared their SUV to a rhinoceros.) Then, ask them to each bring in two examples of metaphors in advertisements for the next class. Spend class time analyzing and discussing the metaphorical relationships in their example ads, and talk about their favorites. Which examples are most effective and why?

- Ask students to practice connecting two dissimilar objects or concepts in as many ways possible. Present them with a list of various objects and a list of various concepts. Have them choose one from each list. Ask them to begin by brainstorming a list of as many similarities or relationships as they can think of for their two list items. Then ask them to create a metaphor from their brainstorming (could be anything from an ad to a photograph to a video to a poem).

- Ask students to brainstorm a problem they face as students on your campus. Then, work as a class to brainstorm solutions that focus on divergent thinking. Emphasize to students that divergent thinking requires us to temporarily censor the critic in our minds (the one that would say, "That won't work!"). Do not rule out any solution, no matter how outlandish. Practice this frequently as a class.

- Require students to participate in regular divergent thinking sessions which ask them to think of as many ideas as possible in a short amount of time (for example, they could engage in an exercise like the 30 Circles Challenge, which requires making circles into as many recognizable objects as possible in a short period of time; this and other ideas can be found on the blog for IDEO, https://www.ideo.com/blog).

Finally, many students are fearful of failure and also of tackling design problems when a solution or path forward is unclear. The ability to face a challenging problem without being weighed down by unease about succeeding is crucial to the practice of creativity. Santos and McIntyre (2016) refer to this "discomfort" and uncertainty inherent in the creative process as "disequilibrium" and argue that designing coursework that pushes students to work within this disequilibrium is a critical part of teaching creativity. Here are some ideas for how to accomplish this in secondary and postsecondary classrooms:

- Assign students problem-based design exercises. To encourage radical imagination, students may be asked to perform a thorough examination of the problem, and then create three probable solutions—one as the slightly improved version of the current resolution, one as the conservative new direction, and one as the revolutionary idea unconstrained by existing realities. Through the collaborative process of choosing a workable solution as a class, students have the opportunity to practice persistence and become comfortable with failure in a safe space.

- Encourage students to engage in written reflections at the conclusion of the design process and to assess challenges and how they were managed. For excellent reflection questions and a more thorough discussion of this approach, see Santos and McIntyre (2016).

■ References and Recommended Readings

Acar, S. & Runco, M. A. (2019). Divergent thinking: New methods, recent research, and extended theory. *Psychology of Aesthetics, Creativity, and the Arts, 13*(2), 153–158.

Andreason, N. (2014). Secrets of the creative brain. *The Atlantic.* https://www.theatlantic.com/magazine/archive/2014/07/secrets-of-the-creative-brain/372299/?utm_campaign=brainfood&utm_medium=email&utm_source=farnamstreet.org.

Csikszentmihalyi, M. (2013). Creativity: Flow and the psychology of discovery and invention. HarperCollins.

Fyffe, S. & Lee, K. (2016, January 19). *How design thinking improves the creative process.* Insights by Stanford Business. https://www.gsb.stanford.edu/insights/how-design-thinking-improves-creative-process.

Hennessey, E. & Mueller, J. (2020). Teaching and learning design thinking (DT): How do educators see DT fitting into the classroom? *Canadian Journal of Education, 43*(2), 499–521.

Hokanson, B. (2006). Creativity in the design curriculum. *Journal of Visual Literacy, 26*(1), 41–52.

Hsiao, S. W., Wang, M. F. & Chen, C. W. (2017). Time pressure and creativity in industrial design. *International Journal of Technology and Design Education, 27*(2), 271–289.

Kaufman, S. B. & Gregoire, C. (2015). *Wired to create.* Random House.

Kelley, D. & Kelley, T. (2013). Creative confidence: Unleashing the creative potential within us all. Crown Business.

Lee, J., Jung, Y. & Yoon, S. (2019). Fostering group creativity through design thinking projects. *Knowledge Management and E-Learning, 11*(3), 378–392.

Oliver, M. (2003). Yes! No! *Owls and other fantasies: Poems and essays* (p. 27). Beacon Press.

Poutanen, P. (2013). Creativity as seen through the complex systems perspective. *Interdisciplinary Studies Journal, 2*(3), 207–221.

Robinson, K. (2017). *Out of our minds: Learning to be creative.* John Wiley & Sons Ltd.

Runco, M. A. (2003). Creativity. *Annual Review of Psychology, 55*, 657–687.

Santos, M. C. & McIntyre, M. M. (2016). Toward a technical communication made whole: Disequilibrium, creativity, and postpedagogy. *Composition Forum, 33.* https://compositionforum.com/issue/33/techcomm.php.

Seelig, T. (2012). inGenius: A crash course on creativity. HarperOne.

Stuhlfaut, M. W. & Windels, K. (2015). The Creative Code: A moderator of divergent thinking in the development of marketing communications. *Journal of Marketing Communications, 21*(4), 241–259.

Zhong, X. M. & Fan, K. K. (2016). A new perspective on design education: A "Creative Production-Manufacturing Model" in "The Maker Movement" context. *EURASIA Journal of Mathematics, Science & Technology Education, 12*(5), 1389–1398.

Zidulka, A. & Kajzer, M. I. (2018). Creativity or cooptation? Thinking beyond instrumentalism when teaching design thinking. *Journal of Management Education, 46*(6), 749–760.

12. Critical Making

Shannon Butts
UNIVERSITY OF FLORIDA

Definition and Background

Critical making is a practice that unites critical thinking and hands-on experiments to encourage learning by doing. Drawing from constructionist approaches to project-based learning, critical making explores the relationships between technologies, art, design, and social issues by making things. According to Matt Ratto (2011), critical making aims "to use material forms of engagement with technologies to supplement and extend critical reflection and, in doing so, to reconnect our lived experiences with technologies to social and conceptual critique" (n.p.).

Critical making unites two sometimes disconnected modes of inquiry—critical thinking and material production. Often, critical thinking describes abstract, internal, linguistically based modes of analysis. In contrast, making generally refers to goal-driven, embodied, material production that focuses on creating a working *prototype*. However, designers critically engage with ideas, and thinkers use material experimentation to work out concepts. Critical making acknowledges an intertwined process that links object-making to academic scholarship and theory-based practices. In making prototypes, iterating on designs, and experimenting with technologies, makers often learn more about the theories, concepts, and innovative possibilities of technical and professional communication. Originally a pedagogical practice, critical making has been adapted as a research program, method of inquiry, and a methodology that continues to shape emerging research practices.

Although the term *critical making* gained popularity in 2009 (Ratto, 2011), the DNA of the critical making process is woven throughout the history of design thinking and technical communication. As mentioned in the introduction of this collection, the mid-twentieth-century origins of design as a science emerged in response to growing social and environmental needs (Fuller, 2019). However, designers often encountered "wicked problems" that resisted clear definitions or formulaic solutions (Rittel & Webber, 1973, p. 160). Design as a discipline shifted towards a more user-centered approach that works out problems by making things—bringing together doing and thinking in the iterative design thinking process.

Similarly, technical communicators have always been "reflective problem-solvers"—working with multiple tools, technologies, cultures, and materials to "identify and solve corporate problems" while also developing innovative solutions to both corporate and social issues (Johnson-Eilola & Selber, 2013, p. 3; Hailey et al., 2010, p. 139). Technical and professional communication (TPC) emphasizes user-centered design thinking that challenges a "one-size fits all"

DOI: https://doi.org/10.37514/TPC-B.2022.1725.2.12

approach. Like critical making, TPC promotes design as a process that changes to address diverse social, ethical, material, and environmental situations.

Design thinking, TPC, and critical making each focus on complex problem-solving, social awareness, and an iterative process of doing and thinking. However, critical making places more emphasis on process, shifting the focus from problem-solving or completing deliverables to the learning process that occurs as participants engage new socio-technical literacies. Rather than a specific design format or method, critical making highlights what you can learn from the practice of design.

■ Design Application

With regard to technical communication, critical making is similar to what Liza Potts (2015) describes as "experience architecture," an "emerging practice that draws together issues of information design, information architecture, interaction design, and *usability* studies to assess and build products, services, and processes" (p. 256, emphasis added). However, instead of focusing on end products or deliverables, critical making emphasizes the making process. Critical making does not always begin with a set research question or end with a textual report. Instead, making practices often challenge usability and work with *failure* as a part of the research process. Critical making emphasizes the embodied acts of making as key to *iterative* design, where participants can explore how changes to design, methods, and materials not only solve problems, but also invite questions like "What happens if . . . ?"

Similar to practices of critical/speculative design (Dunne & Raby, 2013) or *participatory design*, the hands-on practice of critical making usurps the production of "effective" or "comfortable" *user-centered design* (Opel & Rhodes, 2018) and often works to translate social or political questions into a material form in order to demonstrate the complex relationships between technology and society. Through critical making, designers and scholars can experiment with alternative approaches, materials, and goals—learning by doing while also acknowledging the many different users, networks, and environments that change how a product (or process) might work. As such, definitions of critical making vary because the process changes with each project or inquiry.

For example, at the 2018 "Control the Controller" workshop in Rotterdam, participants deconstructed and reassembled game and remote controllers to learn more about how mechanics mediate human-computer interaction (Groten & van der Kooij, 2018). Buttons, scrolling bars, gestures, even voice commands assume a type of access and ability, and the mechanisms control how people can engage various technologies. In breaking down the material components of a controller, the participants can evaluate assumptions about access and consider how design affects communication and engagement. In addition, participants were able to draft innovative new designs and brainstorm about how different tools or access methods might appeal to different communities. The critical making process creates opportunities to understand not just technical aspects, but how technologies shape social, cultural, political, and economic values.

■ Pedagogical Integration

In part, critical making emerged in response to the widespread popularity of maker movements and the growing availability of digital tools through the Internet of Things. The development of Web 2.0 alongside advances in digital tools such as 3D printing, CAD software, and Arduino microcontrollers (to name a few) created new communities of makers tinkering with technology. As more people started to participate in digital design and fabrication, scholars across disciplines such as information technology, writing, design, engineering, and communication began to investigate how to critically use these new tools for more than "copy, paste, make" (Dunne, A. & Raby, F., 2013; Hertz, 2012; Oliver et al., 2011; Purdy, 2014; Ratto, 2011; Ratto et al., 2014; Sengers et al., 2005).

While DIY collectives and maker labs continue to encourage people to "make stuff," critical making encourages people to consider why, how, and to what effect making impacts society. According to Matt Ratto (2011), critical making aims "to use material forms of engagement with technologies to supplement and extend critical reflection and, in doing so, to reconnect our lived experiences with technologies to social and conceptual critique" (n.p.). Critical makers are not merely interested in creating a prototype and singling out the technical. Instead, instructors may encourage a social-science approach that balances the technical with the social and advocates for making interventions into emerging technical landscapes. As Jason Tham (2021) notes, critical making and design thinking encourage innovative approaches to problem-solving that promote critical reflection and *social justice* advocacy. Through making things, students can learn more about how tools and technologies shape technical and professional communication and ultimately influence meaning making practices.

A signature application of critical making in the classroom is the design challenge exercise. A design challenge presents its participants with a complex social problem and requires them to ideate and prototype radical solutions with the goal of *testing* them outside the lab at a later stage. While the traditional design challenge focuses on the effectiveness of the final solution, the critical design challenge steers the participants' attention from the so-called practical aspects of design—i.e., costs, supplies, viability—to the critical dimensions of *ethics*, social justice, and user advocacy. Participants have opportunities to collaborate, work through the wicked problems associated with design, and experiment with diverse problem-solving methods. This approach can be integrated into technical and professional communication instruction where students tackle complex social problems from the communicative standpoint.

Increasingly, technical and professional communicators tinker with technologies to figure out how to best design and deliver information. These jobs are "no longer just about translating complex technical information for everyday users but instead solving problems through communication and material resources" (Tham, 2021, p. 2). Critical making challenges technical and professional communicators to pay attention to both product and process and better understand the social aspects of iterative design practices. Technical communicators play a key role in framing how users interact with content and engage technologies (Swarts, 2020). They have to consider content strategy, user experience, accessibility, community engagement, market needs and **constraints**, as well as the social and technical components that will affect communication. The "what happens if" questions of critical making help communicators develop innovative approaches that add value to professional environments. Whether composing a professional document or building a video game, a critical making approach encourages communicators to consider not just format, content, or tools, but also workflow, **collaborative** opportunities, and how to package information to make an impact.

■ References and Recommended Readings

Boler, M. & Ratto, M. (2014). DIY citizenship: *Critical making and social media*. MIT Press.

D'Ignazio, C. (2017). What would feminist data visualization look like? https://visions carto.net/feminist-data-visualization.

DiSalvo, C. (2012). *Adversarial design*. MIT Press.

Dunne, A. & Raby, F. (2013). *Speculative everything: Design, fiction, and social dreaming*. MIT Press.

Fuller, R. B. (2019). *Utopia or oblivion: The prospects for humanity*. Lars Müller Publishers.

Groten, A. & van der Kooij, H. (2018, June 28). Control the controller [Workshop]. Thursday Night Live! Het Nieuwe Instituut, Rotterdam, the Netherlands. https:// thursdaynight.hetnieuweinstituut.nl/en/activities/anja-groten-heerko-van-der-kooij -control-controller.

Hailey, D., Cox, M. & Loader, E. (2010). Relationship between innovation and professional communication in the "creative" economy. *Journal of Technical Writing and Communication, 40*(2), 125–141.

Hertz, G. (2012). *Critical making*. Telharmonium Press. http://conceptlab.com/critical making/ .

Hertz, G. (2016). What is critical making? *Current, 7*. http://current.ecuad.ca/what-is -critical-making.

Johnson-Eilola, J. & Selber, S. A. (2013). *Solving problems in technical communication*. University of Chicago Press.

Oliver, J., Savičić, G. & Vasiliev, D. (2011). *The critical engineering manifesto*. http:// criticalengineering.org.

Opel, D. & Rhodes, J. (2018). Beyond student as user: Rhetoric, multimodality, and user-centered design. *Computers and Composition, 49*, 71–81.

Potts, L. (2015). Archive experiences: A vision for user-centered design in the digital humanities. In J. Ridolfo & W. Hart-Davidson (Eds.), *Rhetoric and the digital humanities* (pp. 255–263). University of Chicago Press.

Purdy, J. (2014). What can design thinking offer writing studies? *College Composition and Communication, 65*(4), 612–641.

Ratto, M. (2011). Critical making: Conceptual and material studies in technology and social life. *The Information Society, 27*(4), 252–260.

Ratto, M., Jalbert, K. & Wylie, S. (2014). Introduction to the special forum on critical making as research program. *The Information Society, 30*(2), 85–95.

Ratto, M. & Ree, R. (2012) Materializing information: 3D printing and social change. *First Monday, 17*(7). https://firstmonday.org/ojs/index.php/fm/article/view/3968/3273.

Rittel, H. W. J. & Webber, M. M. (1973). Dilemmas in a general theory of planning. *Policy Sciences, 4*(2), 155–169.

Sengers, P., Boehner, K., David, S. & Kaye, J. J. (2005). Reflective design. In *Proceedings of the 4th decennial conference on Critical computing: Between sense and sensibility* (pp. 49–58). ACM.

Swarts, J. (2020). Technical communication is a social medium. *Technical Communication Quarterly, 29*(4), 427–439.

Tham, J. (2021). *Design thinking in technical communication: Solving problems through making and collaboration.* Routledge.

13. Design Ethics

Rachael Sullivan
SAINT JOSEPH'S UNIVERSITY

Definition and Background

Design ethics refers to practical standards that professional designers follow, such as copyright law, conflict of interest policies, licensing and legal protections, and federal regulations surrounding accessibility. Design organizations across the world publish codes or guidelines outlining ethical conduct for professional designers (Perkins, 2006). Yet, ethical design entails much more than following rules. It is the result of negotiating complex networks of human and non-human actors, as well as acknowledging systems of inequality and oppression, both internal and external to the design profession. In this more capacious definition of design ethics, we find a mindset that searches for implications beyond those that typically surface in institution- or client-driven orientations.

In creating an ethical design, designers and communicators are accountable to the larger social, environmental, political, and economic contexts in which the design will circulate, and they consider the potential consequences of what they create. As Nick Monteiro (2017) put it, "Asking ourselves why we are making something is an infinitely better question than asking ourselves whether we *can* make it." Ethical design practices may address a range of intersecting *social justice* issues, such as the future of the planet (Chan, 2018), human rights (Harihareswara, 2015), racial justice (Benjamin, 2019), gender diversity (Edenfield, 2019), labor hierarchies (Suchman, 1995), disability (Hamraie, 2013), or intercultural differences (Sun, 2012). Approaches such as *participatory design*, *user-centered design*, *social design*, inclusive design, sustainable design, and feminist design overlap with design ethics. Technical communication scholars have explored design ethics in varied contexts; document design, in particular, has provided a rich site for inquiry about power relations and the designer's ethical responsibility (Dragga, 1996; Edenfield, 2019; Herrington, 1995; Jarrett et al., 2014).

The need for ethics in design may seem obvious. As Ashanka Kumari notes in her entry on *equity*, today's design thinkers readily acknowledge that the made-world reflects biases, power, and privilege. However, many working in industrial and graphic design when these were nascent fields in the 1950s and 1960s actively ignored social contexts and presumed objectivity and neutrality in their work. The deeper ethical concerns that fuel design activism and advocacy today arose from social movements in the 1960s, 1970s, and 1980s, which brought awareness to major global challenges. Writing about this period, Clive Dilnot (1984) observed a shift in the design profession's approach to ethics—a move from looking inward

DOI: https://doi.org/10.37514/TPC-B.2022.1725.2.13

towards the client and the profession to looking outward, towards "the wider social world that produces the determining circumstances within which designers work" (p. 244). Throughout the 1980s and 1990s, designers continued to consider diverse audiences and interests that were not purely (at least on the surface) commercial. In 1994 for example, Katherine McCoy invoked design as a form of activism: "We cannot be passive anymore. Designers must be good citizens and participate in the shaping of our environment" (p. 212).

In conceptualizing "design ethics" as social responsibility and not just professional responsibility, this chapter emphasizes *inclusion* and commitment to the public good as critical values in user research, design, and decision-making. For this reason, design thinking is sometimes viewed as an ethical approach to design because of the focus on real-world situations, empathy, and diverse stakeholders. However, a design ethics lens may reveal problems with "design thinking" itself. For instance, Lilly Irani (2018) has argued that the embrace of design thinking in North America is characterized by exclusionary, market-oriented labor hierarchies, as well as racialized and gendered definitions of what counts as "technology" and "expertise." The concept of *empathy*, the first phase in the design thinking process, also has potential to serve exploitative capitalist production and exacerbate asymmetries of power. As the anthropologist and user researcher Sekai Farai (2020) cautions, colonial desire for domination may filter into design thinking and commercial design industries more broadly through the "trojan horse" of empathy. Designers and user researchers who identify with overrepresented groups and who separate themselves from users (rather than form relationships and coalitions) struggle with empathetic practice. Design ethics requires those with privilege to practice radical self-awareness and develop empathy over time and with intention (Farai, 2020).

∎ Design Application

Design ethics offers a framework for thinking through design choices from at least two vantage points—first as practitioners or makers, and second as consumers or users. For example, flawed ballot design in the United States has significant impact on election outcomes, with greater harm done to poor, elderly, and disabled voters (Chisnell, 2016; Norden et al., 2012). From the perspective of ballot designers, they must account for diverse users and uphold their responsibility to the integrity of democratic processes. From the perspective of users (voters), they are presented with an opportunity to critically analyze ballot design, as so many Americans did in the five weeks following the 2000 Gore-Bush presidential election, when confusing ballots in Florida "likely caused more than 2,000 Democratic voters to mistakenly vote for Pat Buchanan" (Norden et al., 2012, p. 21). Similarly, widespread media coverage of Facebook's handling of misinformation and malicious political advertisements during the 2016 presidential election sparked debates about social media platforms' role in facilitating (or weakening) democracy through the design of interfaces and algorithms (Phillips, 2018).

In addition to caring about the public good, putting design ethics into practice also hinges on inclusion. Through inclusive design, the line between expert "designer" and non-expert "user" collapses. Kat Holmes (2018) argued that we must see excluded groups as experts and co-designers; their experience is their strength (pp. 56–57). As an example of this subversion, Avery Edenfield (2019) researched queer approaches to the design of sexual consent information. He demonstrated how "marginalized communities create, communicate, and educate each other" through zines, photocopied flyers, and other forms of "extra-institutional and tactical technical communication" (pp. 4, 10). Here is an example of ethical design: Community-led practices resulted in better outcomes for people who are not part of the dominant group, a conclusion that Sasha Costanza-Chock (2020) reiterates through her influential design justice framework (which also offers many examples of ethical design).

Through these and related approaches, designers are better positioned to work towards collective justice and avoid doing harm. They continuously consider what groups of people *might be left out*, what values or biases *might be operating* more or less visibly, and what relations *will most likely be shaped* between the communicator and the audience as a result of what they make or how they conduct user research.

■ Pedagogical Integration

Instructors may ask students to weigh considerations of purpose and audience across a range of design projects. Students may develop and plan their communication goals in pre-design proposals, as well as reflect on and articulate their rhetorical situation and choices in post-design narratives. These types of written assignments lead to questions about ethical implications: how the students' designs may have both intended and unintended effects, and how they might foresee and avoid inflicting harm with their designs. Beyond simply outlining purpose and audience, a focus on design ethics in pre- and post-design writing may lead to challenging, productive lines of inquiry—perhaps even more valuable for assessment and learning than the final product.

Students may also structure written reflection focused on design ethics through questions about relations and effects, such as those Anne Wysocki and Dennis Lynch (2012) offered in their textbook *Compose, Design, Advocate*:

- "What do you want the world to be? How do we live together well?" (p. 284)
- "Whose lives are not being considered?" (p. 284)
- "Is the project you are considering worthwhile? Will it have real effects through helping others?" (p. 288)
- "What strategies will best help you establish the relations you seek with your audiences and . . . others affected by the problem?" (p. 288)

Although Wysocki and Lynch write within the context of rhetoric and advocacy, these questions apply to many types of technical and professional communication assignments and scenarios. In reviewing current pedagogical approaches to design ethics, Debra Lilley and Vicky A. Lofthouse (2009) have found teaching strategies such as role-play, case studies, and group discussions to be common practices in the classroom. Applied to these strategies, the questions above could prompt students to acknowledge different interest parties and how intersectionality complicates and enriches their design process.

Students could also use or modify the Wysocki and Lynch questions to analyze the ethics of a design that someone else (e.g., a professional designer or a classmate) created. Zarah C. Moeggenberg's entry on **inclusion** establishes the need for designers to engage dynamic, multidimensional perspectives. This work is difficult but necessary for anyone pursuing **equity** in design.

Constantly asking "who or what is being excluded?"—from both the design team *and* the design itself—unearths ethical shortcomings. For example, during the COVID–19 pandemic, the website for crowdsourced design campaign "STAY SANE/STAY SAFE" (2020) featured countless posters imploring viewers to "stay home." Using the Wysocki and Lynch questions above, students might analyze these posters and ask whose lives are *not* being considered: Unhoused people are excluded from this design, as are victims of domestic violence and abuse (to name just a few out of many possible ethical considerations to explore). The campaign does harm by exacerbating the otherness and trauma that displaced and abused people already experience. Following this analysis, students could design their own poster to demonstrate principles of ethical design and address/repair injustice in the context of public health.

■ References and Recommended Readings

Benjamin, R. (2019). *Race after technology: Abolitionist tools for the New Jim Code*. Polity.

Chan, J. K. H. (2018). Design ethics: Reflecting on the ethical dimensions of technology, sustainability, and responsibility in the Anthropocene. *Design Studies, 54*, 184–200. https://doi.org/10.1016/j.destud.2017.09.005.

Chisnell, D. (2016, April 18). *Democracy is a design problem: Election ballot design* [Video]. Design Driven NYC. https://www.youtube.com/watch?v=sGFtTJne8Sk.

Costanza-Chock, S. (2020). *Design justice: Community-led practices to build the worlds we need*. MIT Press.

Dilnot, C. (1984). The state of design history, part I: Mapping the field. *Design Issues, 1*(1), 4–23. https://doi.org/10.2307/1511539.

Dragga, S. (1996). "Is this ethical?" A survey of opinion on principles and practices of document design. *Technical Communication, 43*(3), 255–265.

Edenfield, A. C. (2019). Queering consent: Design and sexual consent messaging. *Communication Design Quarterly, 7*(2), 1–15. https://doi.org/10.1145/3358931.3358938.

Farai, S. (2020, June). *The impossibility and irrelevance of empathy*. UXRConf. https://joinlearners.com/talk/the-impossibility-and-irrelevance-of-empathy.

Hamraie, A. (2013). Designing collective access: A feminist disability theory of universal design. *Disability Studies Quarterly, 33*(4). http://dsq-sds.org/article/view/3871.

Harihareswara, S. (2015). User experience is a social justice issue. *The Code4Lib Journal*, *28*. http://journal.code4lib.org/articles/10482.

Herrington, T. K. (1995). Ethics and graphic design. *IEEE Transactions on Professional Communication*, *38*(3), 151–157. https://doi.org/10.1109/47.406728.

Holmes, K. (2018). *Mismatch: How inclusion shapes design*. MIT Press.

Irani, L. (2018). Design thinking: Defending Silicon Valley at the apex of global labor hierarchies. *Catalyst: Feminism, Theory, Technoscience*, *4*(1). https://doi.org/10.28968/cftt.v4i1.243.

Jarrett, C., Redish, G. & Summers, K. (2014). Designing for people who do not read easily. In L. Melonçon (Ed.), *Rhetorical accessAbility: At the intersection of technical communication and disability studies* (pp. 39–65). Baywood Publishing.

Lilley, D. & Lofthouse, V. (2009). Sustainable design education—considering design for behavioural change. *Engineering Education*, *4*(1), 29–41. https://doi.org/10.11120/ened.2009.04010029.

McCoy, K. (1994). Countering the tradition of the apolitical designer. In M. Bierut, W. Drenttel, S. Heller & D. Holland (Eds.), *Looking closer 2: Critical writings on graphic design* (pp. 212–224). Allworth Press; American Institute of Graphic Arts.

Monteiro, M. (2017, July 6). *A designer's code of ethics*. Dear Design Student. https://deardesignstudent.com/a-designers-code-of-ethics-f4a88aca9e95.

Norden, L., Quesenbery, W. & Kimball, D. C. (2012). *Better design, better elections*. Brennan Center for Justice, New York University School of Law. https://www.brennancenter.org/sites/default/files/legacy/Democracy/VRE/Better_Design_Better_Elections.pdf.

Perkins, S. (2006). *Ethics and social responsibility*. AIGA. https://web.archive.org/web/20210423134937/https://www.aiga.org/ethics-and-social-responsibility.

Phillips, W. (2018, May). *The oxygen of amplification*. Data & Society. https://datasociety.net/output/oxygen-of-amplification/.

Stay sane / stay safe. (2020). http://stay-sane-stay-safe.com/.

Suchman, L. (1995). Making work visible. *Communications of the ACM*, *38*(9), 56–64. https://doi.org/10.1145/223248.223263.

Sun, H. (2012). *Cross-cultural technology design: Creating culture-sensitive technology for local users*. Oxford University Press.

Wysocki, A. F. & Lynch, D. A. (2012). *Compose, design, advocate* (2nd ed.). Pearson.

14. Digital Fabrication

Emily F. Brooks
UNIVERSITY OF FLORIDA

■ Definition and Background

A unique emphasis of design thinking is the ***prototyping*** phase. A prototype is a preliminary theoretical artifact that can be tested before polished and finalized. In maker culture and design thinking writ large, to materialize a theoretical artifact is to fabricate its existence. Digital fabrication is a popular method to materialize an idea and make a prototype digitally. Digital fabrication is an umbrella term that describes design and making processes that require digital modeling and manufacturing tools to create material outputs. With the proliferation of hobbyist digital fabrication technologies across workplaces and learning institutions, non-expert designers are afforded the opportunity to design and create prototypes of creative products at a low cost. Hobbyist fabrication is often celebrated as a motivator for professional undertaking. Personal interests in certain issues in the world can lead to innovative projects supported by institutions. The "20% time" method (also known as side-project time), made famous by Google, is one of such examples. Google employees were encouraged to spend 20 percent of their paid working time on something they thought would benefit the company and the world (Clark, 2021). Digital fabrication is a staple exercise in these experimental projects. The three main types of digital fabrication are 3D additive (3D printing), 2D subtractive (laser cutting), and 3D subtractive (CNC milling).

■ 3D Additive –

The term *3D printing* is typically used to describe rapid 3D plastic prototyping, often generating a smaller scale model using cheaper materials until the design is settled and a mold can be created for mass production in more expensive materials. Typical hobbyist 3D printers function similarly to hot glue guns, except they use plastic filament instead of glue and the nozzle moves with motors on precise XYZ coordinates to build up a composite of slices or layers to create a cohesive model. The most common plastics used in 3D printing are PLA (polylactic acid), which is more biodegradable and creates less toxic fumes, and ABS (acrylonitrile butadiene styrene) like in toy bricks, which is much sturdier. In addition to plastics, makers have tinkered with 3D printing in typical materials like resin, clay, and metals, as well as more unconventional materials like chocolate, cheese, and pancake batter. 3D prints are made from 3D models in file types like STL (stereolithographic) or OBJ (object) from computer-aided design (CAD) software,

DOI: https://doi.org/10.37514/TPC-B.2022.1725.2.14

which range from those for amateur hobbyists to those for professional artists and engineers. Some websites offer free or paid models to download and print. 3D printers come in a wide range, from hobby to professional, and many can now be found in university libraries and makerspaces.

▌ 2D Subtractive –

Laser cutting is often used to cut out pieces or add etched designs to usually flat materials like wood or plexiglass/acrylic, although the technology has become advanced to where one can laser cut pretty much anything, even toast and cookies. Laser cutters require digital design files that specify cut (vector) or etch (raster), and the laser cutting machine can vary the speed and power of the laser to affect the depth of the cut. Designers typically want to output an SVG (scalable vector graphics) file from design software, which provides precise coordinates of paths to cut out the final design. Laser cutters produce toxic fumes and are a fire hazard so are usually not found in libraries, but they can be found in fabrication laboratories (fab labs). Crafters can also cut thinner materials like paper, cardstock, and vinyl using computer-aided design vinyl cutters that likewise accept vector files and can be found in libraries and makerspaces.

▌ 3D Subtractive –

CNC (computer numerical control) mills or routers are advanced tools used to cut out a design from a pre-existing material, rather than build up from scratch. CNC milling can cut through plywood, plastic, foam board, and even metal to create a 3D design from a specific computer code. These are expensive machines and are only occasionally found in makerspaces.

▌ Design Application

Digital fabrication is often used in *rapid prototyping*, usually at a smaller or less expensive scale than the intended final result. Designers may preliminarily sketch ideas, but may also require material, dimensional prototypes to determine the feasibility and *usability* of the idea. Design thinking requires *creativity* as to the *affordances* and *constraints* of available technologies, but also consideration of material impact. For example, when hospitals faced a shortage of personal protective equipment during the COVID–19 pandemic, many makers joined the efforts with digital fabrication. 3D-printed plastic N95 masks did not work well as they could not create a tight, but breathable seal like the typical fabric, but Columbia University researchers were able to 3D print face shields and headbands (Gil & Trinidad-Christensen, 2020). Makers at Georgia Institute of Technology also used laser cutting to cut acrylic face shields (Toon, 2020). While digital fabrication is a technology, a tool, and a medium, it can also be an object of critique, especially in *critical making*. 3D printing melting plastics or burning acrylics with lasers in themselves invoke design problems in terms of workplace toxicity and ethics of global warming, as do problems of *equity* and access to digital fabrication resources. The generation of waste plastic has led to creative recycling ventures, where the filament is melted down and re-extruded (Gonzalez & Bennett, 2016). Digital fabrication is most often tied to technical communication in terms of multimodal composition.

■ Pedagogical Integration

Scholars are using digital fabrication in pedagogy and in research to materialize concepts. For example, Aaron Santesso (2017) from Georgia Institute of Technology assigned his students to laser cut Renaissance style medallions inspired by the literature they were reading. As a Ph.D. student, Jonathan Fitzgerald (2015) from Northeastern University laser cut a complicated interwoven Early Modern pattern poem by an anonymous poet that he discovered on the EEBO (Early English Books Online) database. While at the University of Florida, I assigned my students to create 3D-printed tactile picture books for non-sighted children and share their instructions with the online maker community, Instructables (2018). A team at the Speculative Sensation Lab (2015) at Duke University created a project that captured the content of scattered cookie crumbs and translated the data into coordinates for a MakerBot 3D printer, creating abstract data creatures. Tiffany Chan (2018) from the University of Victoria reverse-engineered a 3D-printed printmaking plate from a 19th century illustration. While the learning curve might be daunting, many students are eager to learn new emerging technologies to help set themselves apart in a competitive career market and often comment how rewarding it is to have a tangible artifact at the end to show their peers.

Though certainly not ubiquitous, the diminished cost of 3D printing has made it a popular trend in DIY and maker culture as well as education. Just as kids learn spatial awareness through playing with dough, 3D modeling and printing connects one's understanding of virtual 3D space on a computer screen with a material 3D result. Replicating 3D objects used to be only for those who had mastered a craft or created a mold, but 3D printing allows for tinkering and generating small-scale models quickly to demonstrate 3D concepts. Some pedagogical implications of digital fabrication are teaching the design process through trial and error, revealing the importance of tactility in a visually dominant culture, and understanding familiar concepts through new perspectives.

For technical and professional communication, digital fabrication offers the opportunity for students to try materializing abstract ideas into tangible, testable models. In this process, students may learn to consider the *affordances* and *constraints* of material resources. Students can also practice *testing* the *usability* of their solution with the fabricated prototypes. As John Sherrill (2014) argued, these learning instances teach students about post-industrial configurations of product design, information exchange, and demonstrating ideas in technical communication. Data physicalization (constructing data with physical objects) also offers opportunities to communicate complex data like sequential trends over time using three dimensions to enhance accessibility, as seen in Rebecca Sutton Koeser et al. (2020) 3D-printed lollipop chart. In essence, digital fabrication offers opportunities to prototype, represent, and communicate in 3D space.

■ References and Recommended Readings

Burgess, H. J. & Rieder, D. M. (2015). Kits, plans, schematics. *Hyperrhiz: New Media Cultures, 13*. http://hyperrhiz.io/hyperrhiz13/.

Clark, D. (2021, December 16). *Google's "20% rule" shows exactly how much time you should spend learning new skills—and why it works*. CNBC Make It. https://www.cnbc.com /2021/12/16/google-20-percent-rule-shows-exactly-how-much-time-you-should -spend-learning-new-skills.html#:~:text=Enter%3A%20Google's%20%E2%80%9 C20%25%20time,wrote%20in%20their%20IPO%20letter.

Cutcher-Gershenfeld, J., Gershenfeld, A. & Gershenfeld, N. (2018). Digital fabrication and the future of work. *Perspective on Work*, 8–13. http://cba.mit.edu/docs/papers /19.01.POW.pdf.

Fitzgerald, J.D. (2015). Re-presenting early modern pattern poems as material objects. https://jonathandfitzgerald.com/blog/2015/05/05/re-presenting-early-modern -pattern-poems-as-material-objects.html.

Georgia Tech. (2017). *Aaron Santesso's literature course in which students make things re- ceives innovative course design award*. https://www.iac.gatech.edu/news-events /stories/2017/12/aaron-santesso-literature-course-students-make-things-receives -innovative-design/599708.

Gil, A. & Trinidad-Christensen, J. (2020). *Guide and design for rapidly produced face shield*. Columbia University Libraries Studio. https://studio.cul.columbia.edu/face-shield/.

Gonzalez, S. A. R. & Bennett, D. B. (2016). *3D printing: A practical guide for librarians*. Rowman and Littlefield.

Instructables. (2018). *3D printed children's tactile book*. http://emilyfbrooks.com/docu ments/3D-Printed-Childrens-Tactile-Book.pdf.

Koeser, R. S., Doroudian, G., Budak, N. & Li, X. (2020). Data beyond vision. *Startwords, 1*. https://doi.org/10.5281/zenodo.4139781.

Northeastern University Libraries. (2015). *3D printed poems, propellers, and more. . . .* https://library.northeastern.edu/sites/default/files/public/atttachments/FIELD_ PAGE_FILES/2015/2015_supporters_newsletter_0.pdf.

Pink, D. (2011). Drive: The surprising truth about what motivates us. Riverhead Books.

Sayers, J. (2015a). Prototyping the past. *Visible Language, 49*(3). https://jntry.work/ptp/.

Sayers, J. (2015b). Why fabricate? *Scholarly and Research Communication, 6*(3). https:// src-online.ca/index.php/src/article/view/209/428.

Sayers, J. (Ed.). (2017). *Making things and drawing boundaries: Experiments in the digital humanities*. University of Minnesota Press.

Sherril, J. T. (2014). *Makers: Technical communication in post-industrial participatory communities* [Doctoral dissertation, Purdue University]. Open Access Theses. https:// docs.lib.purdue.edu/open_access_theses/378.

Speculative Sensation (S–1) Lab, Duke University. (2015). Manifest data: A kit to create personal digital data-based sculptures. *Hyperrhiz: New Media Cultures, 13.* http://hyperrhiz.io/hyperrhiz13/sensors-data-bodies/manifest-data.html .

Toon, J. (2020). *Do-it-yourself medical devices and protective gear fuel battle against COVID–19.* Georgia Tech. https://news.gatech.edu/2020/03/23/do-it-yourself-medical-devices-and-protective-gear-fuel-battle-against-covid-19.

University of Victoria. (2018, February 1). *Adventures in 3D print(mak)ing: From 2D to 3D and back.* https://onlineacademiccommunity.uvic.ca/dsc/2018/02/01/adventures-in-3d-printmaking-from–2d-to–3d-and-back/ .

15. Edge Cases

Mary E. Caulfield
MASSACHUSETTS INSTITUTE OF TECHNOLOGY

Definition and Background

Designers need to anticipate the ways a system will be used, not only to optimize user experience, but also to ensure that a design functions as intended without catastrophic failure. The term *edge cases* is used to describe uses of the product that are not prohibited but fall outside the mainstream of expected use. Designs are also structured around intended use, anticipating failures or hazards that emerge in ways that are not always obvious. In computer-based systems, engineers may anticipate the peak processing loads a system will undergo while still functioning as the customer or user expects. Structural engineers design for peak loads, weather conditions, and other factors that will affect the life of a piece of equipment, building, bridge, or its component materials. Increasingly, social justice concerns have revealed that the profile of a user is too narrow and that use cases do not account for cultural or environmental differences. The study of edge cases is of particular interest in technical and professional communication (TPC) because the analysis of these cases requires diverse perspectives in order to anticipate the context in which a product will be used.

Edge cases refer to unusual use conditions, stresses, or potential for harm that fall outside the expected use of the system. These cases are rare, but the design should function when they occur. Even in innovative or "next generation" products, a system should respond in ways that do not cause loss of life, loss of data, or loss of property to the user, the customer, or other stakeholders. While designers may specify parameters or conditions under which a product or system may be used, it is desirable for systems to exceed those specifications. In projects with a defined customer or client, design teams often devise a user contract, which outlines the intended use of a device and the types of stresses it will be exposed to.

Design Application

Design has become increasingly complex and interdisciplinary. While the term *edge cases* is often understood to apply to computer systems, design pedagogy is applied to a wide variety of technical courses in engineering and the sciences. Design pedagogy is taught in such courses as medical device design, materials science, and chemical engineering project labs that focus on the creation of biofuels and the manufacture of vaccines. All of these classes require a combination of

DOI: https://doi.org/10.37514/TPC-B.2022.1725.2.15

technical knowledge, empathy for users, and understanding of the ethical impacts an innovative design may have on the community and the environment.

Edge cases are considered from two perspectives: peak stresses and user interaction. In the case of peak conditions, worst-case scenarios are evaluated and tested. These worst-case scenarios may be situations such as high demand for network usage, catastrophic weather conditions, disasters, or "perfect storm" scenarios in which a combination of unusual phenomena occur at the same time. In cases where failures occur, the aim of designers is to have the system fail in ways that can be predicted or from which stakeholders can recover. When evaluating user interaction, designers observe the behavior of a wide range of customers or users that make up the audience for a product or system. Edge case audiences may be defined as having physical or cognitive limitations; lack of familiarity with the technology, language, or culture; or they may adapt a product in a way that differs slightly from—but does not violate—the conditions in the customer contract.

■ Pedagogical Integration

As user profiles and user stories evolve, awareness of edge cases becomes an opportunity for collaboration between designers with a variety of technical backgrounds and perspectives on users' encounters with devices and technology. Design education aims to teach habits of projecting, through techniques such as quantitative modeling, resilient design, and study of previous catastrophic failures—the scenarios in which design can fail. In his thesis for an MFA at Iowa State, Edward Cupps (2014) noted that, while design education emphasizes anticipating problems, the process for making predictions has become increasingly complex. Understanding a diverse body of conditions, *prototyping*, and *testing* recursively are part of a method that should be taught to design students. In design pedagogies such as MIT's Design of Medical Devices and Massachusetts College of Art and Design's class in Design Research, exploring edge cases of high functionality and *usability* are an intrinsic part of the work on the final design project.

In a TPC course, instructors may assign students the exercise of designing edge cases by considering general versus extreme user scenarios. First, ask students to choose a mobile live-casting application (e.g., YouTube, Vimeo, Periscope, Meerkat) or any specific services of interest. Then, identify the general user base and user requirements (e.g., setting their location, scheduling livecasts, generating fanbase, managing comments, monetizing broadcasts). Once students have a general understanding of the likely interactions that users may have with the app, ask them to sketch a scenario or two where users may experience catastrophic errors or boundary conditions that would make the user quit the app. Have students write those scenarios in a complete story form and then share it with their peers. Ask students how they would react if they found themselves in those edge cases, and then have them generate potential solutions that could be built into the app to debug those extreme scenarios.

Courses that focus on the design of larger, more complex systems may ask students to model the effects of conditions such as catastrophic climate change on materials and structures. Students may also be asked to create computer-based scenarios that show the way a user with physical challenges or assistive devices interacts with a product or system.

■ References and Recommended Readings

Christensen, T. (2019). *Design edge cases and where to find them.* https://tannerchristensen.com/blog/2019/6/17/design-edge-cases-and-where-to-find-them.

Cupps, E. (2014). *Introducing transdisciplinary design thinking in early undergraduate education to facilitate collaboration and innovation* [Master's thesis, Iowa State University]. Graduate theses and dissertations. https://lib.dr.iastate.edu/etd/13941.

Dym, C. (2009). *Engineering design: A project-based introduction.* John Wiley and Sons.

Hall, A. (2011). Experimental design: Design experimentation. *Design Issues, 27*(2), 17–26.

Johnson, J. (2007). *GUI bloopers 2.0: Common user interface design don'ts and dos.* Morgan Kaufmann Publishers.

Lane, L. (2021). Interstitial design process: How design thinking and social design processes bridge theory and practice in TPC pedagogy. In M. Klein (Ed.), *Effective teaching of technical communication: Theory, practice, and application.* The WAC Clearinghouse; University Press of Colorado. https://doi.org/10.37514/TPC-B.2021.1121.2.02.

Slocum, A. (2007). *FUNdaMENTALS of design.* http://pergatory.mit.edu/resources/fundamentals.html.

Spacey, J. (2018). *What is design to the edges?* Simplicable. https://simplicable.com/new/design-to-the-edges.

Tham, J. C. K. (2021). *Design thinking in technical communication: Solving problems through making and collaboration.* Routledge.

16. Entrepreneurship

Jason Luther
ROWAN UNIVERSITY

Definition and Background

Entrepreneurship refers to a set of nonlinear practices and activities that create novel business models for goods or services that are either lacking or nonexistent. In terms of design thinking, entrepreneurs design creative, responsive, or niche solutions to problems within the context of a marketplace. Often, entrepreneurs innovate by exploiting opportunities and searching for sources of new ideas or combinations, especially as they emerge from recurrent problems with existing designs (Spinuzzi, 2016). As such, technical and professional communication (TPC) scholars point to the complex communicative processes, identities, and networks that entrepreneurs engage as they attempt to convince others that their innovations have value. Capacities for opportunity vary depending on an entrepreneur's experiential, social, or technological resources. Hence, scholars have been interested in entrepreneurs' identity formation, including how they discuss risk or failure (Lauren & Pigg, 2016; Williams et al., 2016), and communicate this within and for entrepreneurial communities and networks (Fraiberg, 2017; Jones, 2017), which are often global (Fraiberg, 2021). Entrepreneurs usually have extensive knowledge in the area in which they are innovating and develop solutions through approaches like design thinking and *user-centered design*, using them to create and revise multimodal genres like pitch decks (Spinuzzi et al, 2015) or crowdfunding campaigns (Gerding & Vealey, 2017; Vealey & Gerding, 2016).

Although entrepreneurship often innovates in search of profit, entrepreneurial thinking has led activist entrepreneurs (Davis, 2017) to challenge growth-only models of capitalism, building more progressive or publicly oriented business strategies framed as social or civic entrepreneurship (Peredo & McLean, 2006; Waddock & Post, 1991). TPC scholars have also examined the cultural rhetorics of entrepreneurship. In Natasha Jones' (2017) study of 12 Black business owners, participants achieve rhetorical agency by promoting various narratives that lead to cultural empowerment. And as Steven Fraiberg (2021) notes in a recent special issue of *Journal of Business and Technical Communication* on entrepreneurship and globalization, scholars should more explicitly account for the "translocal systems" of design and innovation happening in cities across the world.

Recent trends in design communities, such as the Maker Movement and open source, offer more complicated entrepreneurial processes. When creators set out to monetize their ideas or objects, they are sometimes described as

DOI: https://doi.org/10.37514/TPC-B.2022.1725.2.16

"digital maker-entrepreneurs" (Troxler & Wolf, 2017) who often arrive at ideas like most entrepreneurs do: through a mix of serendipity and iteration. However, unlike more traditional entrepreneurs, makers often do not possess *a-prioi* expert knowledge, but instead arrive at **innovations** by accessing social and technological resources via makerspaces, websites, and brokering platforms. These spaces not only provide tools and knowledge but also allow for opportunities to emerge through nonlinear and heterogeneous processes, from bringing prototypes to market via digital fabrication and manufacturing tools, like 3D printers, to creating markets that support product creation through crowdfunding or e-commerce sites. Peter Troxler and Patricia Wolf (2017) provide several case studies of digital maker-entrepreneurs who use computer-aided design (CAD) programs to design popular fan art that is then freely shared on sites like Thingiverse, but also 3D printed and sold on Etsy or Amazon.

Since the motives, resources, and social arrangements of makers often differ from more traditional business models, entrepreneurship scholars have looked at the maker movement as a potential model for the future of small businesses and manufacturing. Some have argued that its strong emphasis on failure and iteration can lead to creative, productive approaches to business (Singh, 2018), while others have focused on the ways decentralized communication leads to more dynamic and diverse entrepreneurial teams (Browder et al., 2019). Most famously, Chris Anderson (2012) argued that the barriers of entry for makers are so low and the demand for niche products so high that any creative person can become an entrepreneur and participate in reinventing the industrial economy.

■ Design Application

Dominant narratives of entrepreneurial success often encourage participation. One example of this is the origin story of Square. A small attachment for mobile devices that captures credit card data, Square exploited a common problem in the shared economy by providing small businesses with a new way to access consumer credit. As Anderson (2012) and other sources (Browder et al., 2019; Holm, 2015) tell it, Square was invented because longtime entrepreneur Jim McKelvey recognized a lost opportunity through his own glass-blowing business. Thanks to a makerspace, he was able to develop a prototype that convinced his partner, Twitter co-founder Jack Dorsey, of the hardware necessary for mass-producing the device and allowed him to understand its quirks and problems more intimately. Ten years after its launch, Square is valued at over four billion dollars and competes with older systems of credit capture.

Despite successes like Square's, an important limitation to exploring the entrepreneurial potential of maker communities is the non-commercial orientation of the movement, which emphasizes open source—rather than proprietary—materials. Thus, some scholars look at how and when makers become entrepreneurial and whether the model is sustainable (see Troxler & Wolf,

2017 for discussion of this and additional case studies). Moreover, narratives like Square's mythologize maker successes rather than telling the more complicated story of iteration through design processes. Longer incubation periods and slower breakthroughs are common to makers (Holm, 2015), and clean stories such as Square's can risk masking the necessary steps toward successful design, including *iteration* and *failing*.

■ Pedagogical Integration

Technical and professional communication educators can integrate entrepreneurial thinking into courses in a number of ways. First, instructors might use entrepreneurship as an accessible and recognizable rhetorical situation for TPC that requires students to consider a range of social, economic, and ethical affordances and challenges as they approach design. For Kyle Vealey and Jeffrey Gerding (2016), teaching civic entrepreneurship through crowdfunding showed student-entrepreneurs how to "identify and frame problems, construct stories about these problems as pressing matters of concern, and both develop and maintain ethical relationships with their stakeholders and an increasingly diverse body of investors" (p. 421).

Because entrepreneurship is a process that involves various genres that often mediate between sellers, users, and investors, entrepreneurship pedagogies ought to help students organize within the wider ecologies in which they are working. One heuristic for organizing project-based entrepreneurship is the Business Model Canvas (BMC), which accounts for key partners, activities, resources, value propositions, customer relationships, revenue streams, and more (Hixon & Paretti, 2014).

As the BMC makes clear, stakeholders and investors are not the only audiences for entrepreneurial projects, but the social context of entrepreneurship emphasizes performative genres such as pitch decks or slides, which can be integrated into broader curricula that focus on design thinking. Clay Spinuzzi et al. (2014, 2015) examined how Korean entrepreneurs critically revised pitch decks in response to feedback from stakeholders from target markets, often reusing texts from other professional genres in the process. Students with entrepreneurially focused assignments ought to be given similar opportunities to revise based on peer or stakeholder feedback.

Likewise, instructors might also use the exigencies of pitches to help students develop strategies for venture success. This means fostering an entrepreneurial identity that exudes zeal and gusto, but is also equipped to accept risk and repeated failure. In their study of presentations from student entrepreneurs, Kristen Lucas et al. (2016) found passion assessment to be an integral part of entrepreneurial communication, suggesting that students need to be taught rhetorical and interpretive strategies that can help them assess passion as both entrepreneurs and investors. For entrepreneurs, passion assessment can help them attend more consciously to nonverbal delivery and rhetorical choices in content; for investors, it can help them attend to design or content of the idea rather than performance alone. Such an assessment is particularly useful for pitches and other situations where venture success is too commonly decided by the entrepreneur's pathos alone.

■ References and Recommended Readings

Anderson, C. (2012). *Makers: The new industrial revolution.* Crown Business.

Browder, R. E., Aldrich, H. E. & Bradley, S. W. (2019). The emergence of the maker movement: Implications for entrepreneurship research. *Journal of Business Venturing, 34*(3), 459–476. https://doi.org/10.1016/j.jbusvent.2019.01.005.

Davis, J. (2017). *From head shops to Whole Foods: The rise and fall of activist entrepreneurs.* Columbia University Press. https://doi.org/10.7312/davi17158.

Fraiberg, S. (2021). Introduction to Special Issue on Innovation and Entrepreneurship Communication in the Context of Globalization. *Journal of Business and Technical Communication, 35*(2), 175–184. https://doi.org/10.1177/1050651920979947.

Gerding, J. M. & Vealey, K. P. (2017). When is a solution not a solution? Wicked problems, hybrid solutions, and the rhetoric of civic entrepreneurship. *Journal of Business and Technical Communication, 31*(3), 290–318. https://doi.org/10.1177/1050651917695538.

Hixson, C. & Paretti, M. C. (2014). Texts as tools to support innovation: Using the Business Model Canvas to teach engineering entrepreneurs about audiences. In P. Weiss and P. Werner (Eds.), *2014 IEEE International Professional Communication Conference* (pp. 1–7). DOI 10.1109/IPCC.2014.7020368.

Holm, E. J. V. (2015). Makerspaces and contributions to entrepreneurship. *Procedia: Social and Behavioral Sciences, 195*, 24–31. https://doi.org/10.1016/j.sbspro.2015.06.167.

Jones, N. N. (2017). Rhetorical narratives of black entrepreneurs: The business of race, agency, and cultural empowerment. *Journal of Business and Technical Communication, 31*(3), 319–349. https://doi.org/10.1177/1050651917695540.

Lauren, B. & Pigg, S. (2016). Networking in a field of introverts: The egonets, networking practices, and networking technologies of technical communication entrepreneurs. *IEEE Transactions on Professional Communication, 59*(4), 342–362. https://doi.org/10.1109/TPC.2016.2614744.

Lucas, K., Kerrick, S. A., Haugen, J. & Crider, C. J. (2016). Personal passion vs. perceived passion in venture pitches. *IEEE Transactions on Professional Communication, 59*, 363–378.

Peredo, A. M. & McLean, M. (2006). Social entrepreneurship: A critical review of the concept. *Journal of World Business, 41*(1), 56–65. https://doi.org/10.1016/j.jwb.2005.10.007.

Singh, S. P. (2018). Lessons from the maker movement. *MIT Sloan Management Review; Cambridge, 59*(3), 1–5.

Spinuzzi, C. (2016). Introduction to the Special Issue on Entrepreneurship Communication. *IEEE Transactions on Professional Communication, 59*(4), 316–322. https://doi.org/10.1109/TPC.2016.2607803.

Spinuzzi, C. (2017). Introduction to Special Issue on the Rhetoric of Entrepreneurship: Theories, Methodologies, and Practices. *Journal of Business and Technical Communication, 31*(3), 275–289. https://doi.org/10.1177/1050651917695537.

Spinuzzi, C., Nelson, S., Thomson, K. S., Lorenzini, F., French, R. A., Pogue, G., Burback, S. D. & Momberger, J. (2014). Making the pitch: Examining dialogue and revisions in entrepreneurs' pitch decks. *IEEE Transactions on Professional Communication, 57*(3), 158–181. https://doi.org/10.1109/TPC.2014.2342354.

Spinuzzi, C., Nelson, S., Thomson, K. S., Lorenzini, F., French, R. A., Pogue, G., Burback, S. D. & Momberger, J. (2015). Remaking the pitch: Reuse strategies in entrepreneurs' pitch decks. *IEEE Transactions on Professional Communication, 58*(1), 45–68. https://doi.org/10.1109/TPC.2015.2415277.

Troxler, P. & Wolf, P. (2017). Digital maker-entrepreneurs in open design: What activities make up their business model? *Business Horizons, 60*(6), 807–817. https://doi.org/10.1016/j.bushor.2017.07.006.

Vealey, K. & Gerding, J. (2016). Rhetorical work in crowd-based entrepreneurship: Lessons learned from teaching crowdfunding as an emerging site of professional writing. *IEEE Transactions on Professional Communication, 59*, 407–427.

Waddock, S. A. & Post, J. E. (1991). Social entrepreneurs and catalytic change. *Public Administration Review, 51*(5), 393–401. https://doi.org/10.2307/976408.

Williams, S. D., Ammetller, G., Rodriguez-Ardura, I. & Li, X. (2016). Building a rhetorical perspective on international entrepreneurship: Comparing stories from the United States, Spain and China. *IEEE Transactions on Professional Communication, 59*, 379–397.

17. Equity

Ashanka Kumari

TEXAS A&M UNIVERSITY–COMMERCE

Definition and Background

Equity responds to the impact of systemic outcomes that go beyond an individual's identity; in other words, for design thinkers, equity means "fair and just access to and representation in scientific and technical communication for all stakeholders" (Haas & Eble, 2018, p. 11). To enact equity, spaces and products must be designed to meet the specific needs of an individual or community, recognizing that each individual or community has different resources. Equity differs from equality, wherein issues are addressed by giving all the same resources; equity requires critically addressing the specific needs of populations. The lack of equity in the world historically impacts marginalized populations such as people with disabilities, Black and Latinx people, women, and transgender individuals. For instance, many auditoriums do not have access to the stage from the audience for those who are not able-bodied and/or able to use stairs or climb onto the stage. The practice of adding ramps, lifts, or other modes of access to the stage much after its initial creation reflects the inequity of the original design.

Equity in design begins by looking at existing systems that "unfairly privilege some over others" and asking "questions about what can be done to level the playing field" (Loew, 2018). Design thinking serves not just as a tool for designing products but also a "powerful problem-solving methodology across fields and sectors" (equityXdesign, 2016). Design remains critical to working towards equity in all spaces. Equity-centered design thinking practices emphasize "dismantling systemic oppression and creating solutions to achieve equity for all," a process that requires designers to unpack histories and "unveil power structures [toward opening] a space for relearning" through empathy and humility (Creative Reaction Lab, 2018).

In 2016, the Stanford d.school reimagined their design thinking framework to promote equity by adding two new design nodes: Notice and Reflect. In the Notice phase, designers engage in critical self-reflection; the Reflect phase occurs throughout the design process, promoting transparency through an "Equity Pause," or "a time to share our learning and see what we can do better next time in the service of equity and inclusion" (Clifford, n.d.).

Design Application

Equitable design practices are an ongoing process that can and will evolve based on ever-changing spaces, places, and interfaces. To better pursue equity in design,

DOI: https://doi.org/10.37514/TPC-B.2022.1725.2.17

designers must collaborate with the consumer, user, or community the design will primarily impact. In other words, designers should enact a "design with, not for" approach. This collaboration must occur throughout the process and not simply during the initial thought process, a practice also referred to as "participatory design" (Loew, 2018). For example, Jennifer Bay (2022) offers one teaching case that can operate as an application for a "design with, not for" approach. Specifically, Bay describes a technical and professional communication (TPC) service course redesign at a midwestern research predominantly white institution (PWI) required by upper-level students. Rather than taking on a project-based approach, Bay pivoted to service-learning, asking "students to research and apply approaches to fostering DEI [Diversity, Equity, and Inclusion] in the local community" (p. 216). Partnering with the president of their local city council, Bay and students in her class collaborated to investigate community perceptions on DEI and offer data-based solutions toward making "the city a more inclusive and welcoming place for Black, Indigenous, People of Color (BIPOC) [and] learning how businesses, the city, and other groups might unintentionally make it difficult for BIPOC to feel welcome" (p. 217). This case offers one example for how designers can include the community in thinking toward equitable design across spaces, places, and interfaces rather than making those design decisions without the input of those directly affected. Equity in design requires design thinkers to consider the desirability, feasibility, and viability at the forefront of their framework. Equitable design practices should also consider the keywords *design ethics*, *inclusion*, and *social justice* among applicable concepts.

■ Pedagogical Integration

Designers must recognize their own perspectives and privileges in order to undertake a project equitably. Educators must work to promote community-building and equity in the design of pedagogical spaces so that students can build trust and confidence in collaboration while reflecting on how their positionality, privilege, and power function in specific spaces (Sano-Franchini et al., 2022; Walton et al., 2019). An example of such an approach comes from Jennifer Sano-Franchini et al. (2022), who utilize "Slack, an online collaboration platform, as a pedagogical tool for enacting social justice in the teaching of technical and professional communication (TPC) online" (p. 1). Further, instructors and students alike can take up Sano-Franchini et al.'s (2022) WARM framework to assess "instructional technology in terms of intersectional social justice, community, access, and equity" (p. 9). This framework asks practitioners to consider the impact of a tool on Workflow, Accountability (to conditions of material inequality), Representation, and Multiple modes of expression (Sano-Franchini et al., 2022).

Additionally, resources such as the Harvard Implicit Association test and Creative Reaction Lab's Equity-Centered Community Design Field Guide serve as solid starting points for engaging equity. Within pedagogical settings, equitable design practices may be enacted through learning activities whereby student designers encounter and grapple with equity issues through design projects. For example, students may be assigned to investigate the asymmetries in gender and pay, race and workplace relations, or culture and innovation as a starting point to understanding how traditions and systemic oppression affect individual and collective advancement in social and professional lives. Students may conduct research or perform design experiments where they devise research questions, data collection, and analysis methods that could yield insights regarding the state of (in)equity in their surrounding community or personal conditions.

■ References and Recommended Readings

Bay, J. (2022). Fostering diversity, equity, and inclusion in the technical and professional communication service course. *IEEE Transactions on Professional Communication*, 65(1), 213–225.

buildingcommunityWORKSHOP. (2018, October 2). The practice of building equity through design thinking. *The Field*. https://thefield.asla.org/2018/10/02/the-practice -of-building-equity-through-design-thinking.

Clifford, D. (n.d.). *Resources: Equity-centered design framework. Overview.* Stanford d.school. https://dschool.stanford.edu/resources/equity-centered-design-framework.

Creative Reaction Lab. (2018). *What is equity-centered community design?* https://crxlab .org/our-approach.

Creative Reaction Lab. (n.d.). *Equity-centered community design field guide.* https://www .surveymonkey.com/r/ECCDfieldguidedownload.

equityXdesign. (2016, November 15). Racism and inequity are products of design. They can be redesigned. *Medium*. https://medium.com/equity-design/racism-and -inequity-are-products-of-design-they-can-be-redesigned–12188363cc6a.

Haas, A. M. & Eble, M. (2018). *Key theoretical frameworks: Teaching technical communica- tion in the twenty-first century.* Utah State University Press.

Loew, M. (2018, June 10). Designing with equity. *Medium.* https://medium.com /@madisonloew/designing-with-equity–878db231ffb1.

Project Implicit. (n.d.). Harvard. https://implicit.harvard.edu/implicit/takeatest.html.

Sano-Franchini, J., Jones, A. M., Jr., Ganguly, P., Robertson, C. J., Shafer, L. J., Wagnon, M., Awotayo, O. & Bronson, M. (2022). Slack, social justice, and online technical communication pedagogy. *Technical Communication Quarterly*, advance online publi- cation. https://doi.org/10.1080/10572252.2022.2085809

Walton, R., Moore, K. R. & Jones, N. N. (2019). *Technical communication after the social justice turn: Building coalitions for action.* Routledge.

18. Failing

Stephanie West-Puckett
UNIVERSITY OF RHODE ISLAND

Zarah C. Moeggenberg
METROPOLITAN STATE UNIVERSITY

Definition and Background

Popular maxims like "Nothing succeeds like failure" or "Success is the surest way to kill *creativity*" are predicated on the idea that failure is a necessary part of *innovation*, a catalyst for finding better solutions to problems on both micro- and macro-scales. On one hand, according to Gerard J. Tellis (2013), "Success . . . provides a strong motive to sustain the status quo and resist innovation" (p. 10). On the other, tolerance for—and even *pursuit of*—failure promotes radical risk-taking behaviors that lead to abiding success in fast-paced, dynamic environments. Failing can be defined as performing, creating, designing, and innovating unsuccessfully and is often thought of as a breach between intention and outcome. But failure can also be rewarding if we approach it through the lenses of failing forward and failing sideways.

In Western learning, creating a positive culture around failure is difficult because failure is constructed ontologically as a state of being as opposed to epistemologically as a way of knowing. Failure marks people as derelicts, defeated by a lack of persistence, ability, or intelligence. This ontological violence is an inherent part of formal education; however, Emily Wierszewski (in this collection) notes that while education has brought us to fear failure, we can teach ourselves to embrace and reflect on our own errors and become more creative. By embracing failure, we lean into its affective and cognitive domains. Certainly, failure can occasion frustration, anxiety, or shame, but it can also challenge, motivate, and ignite passion. Failure can reveal insufficiencies in task, process, or problem-solving knowledge, but it can also prompt the development of metacognitive strategies. Moreover, the embrace of failure can strengthen intra- and interpersonal capacities as we become more open and flexible in the design process and seek out others to consult or collaborate with. By leaning into the lessons of failure, we reframe failures as springboards for reaching our goals. In other words, we fail forward. To quote John C. Maxwell (2000), author of the titular book that popularized the term, "failing forward" means "taking responsibility, learning from each mistake, knowing failure is part of progress, maintaining a positive attitude, challenging outdated assumptions, taking new risks, believing something didn't work, [and] persevering" (p. 10).

DOI: https://doi.org/10.37514/TPC-B.2022.1725.2.18

As an alternative to the practice of failing forward, which (eventually) pays dividends through the normative objects of success, we also recognize queer notions of failure which hold promise for *failing sideways*. J. Jack Halberstam (2011) writes of failure as something that offers different rewards, rewards that would not be attainable through success. For Halberstam (2011), failure *is not* indicative of an individual's shortcomings or performance in a given system, nor is it a necessary springboard for achieving traditional markers of success. Halberstam writes, "Failure is something queers do and have always done exceptionally well. . . . In fact, if success requires so much effort [and is always already on someone else's terms], then maybe failure is easier in the long run and offers differing rewards" (2011, p. 3). Failure, as a queer tactic, rejects the expeditious route to success. Historically, technical communication has framed success around the qualities of concision, clarity, accuracy, and coherency. Failing sideways would allow technical communicators to momentarily uncouple their practice from these norms and follow meandering, circuitous—even dead-end—paths that lead to other ways of knowing, being, and making together. As such, failing sideways offers the potential to center bodies, especially those from marginalized communities, in the design process by accounting for a diversity of needs, wants, desires, outcomes, and experiences. Instead of framing the non-normative user as the "trouble" or "failure," failing sideways can restructure normative notions of **usability** and aid designers in becoming advocates who create useable systems, products, and texts for those whose bodies and behaviors don't or won't conform to prescriptive goals or outcomes (Moeggenberg & Walton, 2019; Ramler, 2020).

To put it simply, failure, as traditionally constructed, is a termination of creative processes. Failing forward, on the other hand, reframes failing as an inherent part of an iterative design process that is necessary to bringing designs to fruition. Finally, failing sideways as design praxis troubles the journey toward a predefined end goal or outcome. It expands flattened and linear design processes to follow the bodies and behaviors of diverse users who have histories of failure with normative systems, products, and texts.

■ Design Application

Design thinking is critically informed by failing forward. In other words, failing forward invites different perspectives, processes, movement, and **iterations**. Failing forward requires us to pause and take note of our surroundings, material conditions, assets, influences, and lenses, which is a crucial knowledge-making practice in design communities. To fail forward, designers move beyond the hubris of their previous successes with tools, materials, concepts, or methods. Designers not only apply new approaches, but they scrutinize outcomes, most of which will fail spectacularly. Maxwell (2000) also notes that designers who fail forward pursue quantity over quality, engaging in the **rapid prototyping** of and early feedback to a wide range of design solutions as opposed to investing time and energy into perfecting their singular, most-beloved idea.

Design thinking works best when negative results are produced, or when we understand what does not work—but this is uncomfortable (Bason & Austin, 2019, p. 86). This is why when we more readily formalize failure in design thinking and problem-solving projects, we become both more comfortable to fail in the future and open to what constructive feedback it can give us (Gomoll et al., 2018). It is important that we be open to engaging with our failures. When we acknowledge shortcomings and provide spaces for their safe discussion, this helps us build communities and increase our shared knowledge (Grover et al., 2017, p. 252). In a given project, we often work to find who or what is to blame instead of framing failure as distributed across human and non-human actants in a system (Pflugfelder, 2018, p. 32). It's easy to ignore the failures and move onward (Poggenpohl & Winkler, 2009, p. 107). Ehren Helmut Pflugfelder (2018) urges designers in project management to consider a project's material-discursive elements, as they influence its vulnerabilities and potential for failure (p. 47).

In design thinking—moving iteratively through design stages—one can succeed in the eyes of one participant but fail in the eyes of another. For example, a successful prototype designed for LGBTQ (lesbian, gay, bisexual, transgender/transitioning, questioning) stakeholders may not necessarily be the right fit for LGBTQ stakeholders with disabilities. Or, in the case of the recent acquisition of Twitter by Elon Musk, users of the social media app have voiced serious concerns about the impacts of implementing user authentication as it could compromise privacy and anonymity (Rigot, 2022). Afsaneh Rigot (2022) notes that Twitter's most marginalized users—those who use the app to forward racial justice, to perform a host of marginalized identities, and to find and communicate about abortion access—stand to suffer disproportionately. Rigot reminds us of the importance of actively pursuing these *edge cases* to failure. Failure helps us understand how we may overlook intersectional identities within those whom we should be "designing with" instead of "designing for."

■ Pedagogical Integration

One way to encourage failure-oriented design in technical communication classrooms is to implement alternative grading practices that prompt students to take risks, fail, and sit with the cognitive and affective experience of failure. These experiences may or may not result in successful or useful communication products, but an assessment-for-learning approach privileges process over product and can disrupt the practices of rushing to solution. A host of classroom assessment practices such as contract grading, labor-based grading, specifications grading, and digital badging can make the classroom more amenable to failing forward and failing sideways (Inoue, 2019; Litterio, 2016; Nilson, 2015; West-Puckett,

2016). Lisa Litterio (2016) also found that contract grading in the technical communication classroom "reinforced that writing technical documents is a process that mirrors the collaborative and communicative practices of workplace writing while the writing, rewriting, and negotiating the contract itself is applicable to the writing in their professional lives" (p. 6).

Another way to incorporate failure as pedagogy is to provide students opportunities to engage with diverse stakeholders. Through practices such as user testing, students find out that designs won't meet user needs. Perhaps the student designed for users with disabilities but failed to account for language barriers. We need to address that failure looks differently all the time. Likewise, if we posit questions—like "How do you address a failure like *this*?" or "How do you address a failure like *that*?"—it gives opportunities for students to address failures through additional design thinking, ***collaboration***, revision, and addressing stakeholders directly. Attempting to postulate all of the ways a project can fail, but also discussing how those failures can be capitalized on and addressed, makes failure a rewarding process.

Finally, we can guide students in researching and creating design failure case studies and analyzing those cases through multiple lenses. Pflugfelder (2018) demonstrated this approach by reviewing how technical communicators have assigned blame to the oft-cited Challenger o-ring disaster and offered a new perspective on design failure. Pflugfelder introduces actor-network theory to illustrate the ways that things and texts, materials and discourses become agents that can conflict and contribute to system failure. Applying these lenses can prompt students to interpret failure from multiple perspectives and to understand how different communicators and stakeholders may have misaligned purposes and conceptual frameworks for a design idea that contribute to its failure. By making those diverse and competing paradigms more transparent, technical communication students can learn to anticipate failure as a necessary part of realizing cooperation, coalescence, and coaction.

■ References and Recommended Readings

Bason, C. & Austin, R. D. (2019). The right way to lead: How to help project teams overcome the inevitable inefficiencies, uncertainties, and emotional flare-ups. *Harvard Business Review, 97*(2), 82–91.

Collopy, F. (2019). Why the failure of systems thinking should inform the future of design thinking. *Design Issues, 24*(2), 97–100.

Gomoll, A., Tolar, E., Hmelo-Silver, C. E., Šabanović, S. (2018). Designing human-centered robots: The role of constructive failure. *Thinking Skills and Creativity, 30*, 90–102. https://doi.org/10.1016/j.tsc.2018.03.001.

Grover, S. D., Cook, K. C., Harris, H. S. & DePew K. E. (2017). Immersion, reflection, failure: Teaching graduate students to teach writing online. *Technical Communication Quarterly, 26*(3), 242–255. https://doi.org/10.1080/10572252.2017.1339524.

Halberstam, J. (2011). *The queer art of failure.* Duke University Press.

Inoue, A. B. (2019). *Labor-based grading contracts: Building equity and inclusion in the compassionate writing classroom.* The WAC Clearinghouse; University Press of Colorado. https://doi.org/10.37514/PER-B.2019.0216.

Litterio, L. M. (2016). Contract grading in a technical writing classroom: A case study. *Journal of Writing Assessment, 9*(2), 1–13. https://escholarship.org/uc/item/02q4g1gt.

Maxwell, J. C. (2000). *Failing forward: Turning mistakes into stepping-stones for success.* Thomas Nelson Publishers.

Moeggenberg, Z. C. & Walton, R. (2019). How queer theory can inform design thinking pedagogy. In *SIGDOC '19: Proceedings of the 37th ACM International Conference on the Design of Communication* (pp. 1–9). ACM. https:/rg/10.1145/3328020.3353924 /doi.o.

Nilson, L. (2015). *Specifications grading: Restoring rigor, motivating students, and saving faculty time.* Stylus Publishing.

Pflugfelder, E. H. (2018). Failure matters: Conflicting practices in a high-tech case. *Journal of Technical Writing and Communication, 48*(1), 32–52. https://doi.org/10.1177 /0047281616662984.

Poggenpohl, S. & Winkler, D. R. (2009). Celebrating failure. *Visible Language, 43*(2–3), 104–111.

Ramler, M. (2020). Queer usability. *Technical Communication Quarterly, 30*(4), 345–358. https://doi.org/10.1080/10572252.2020.1831614.

Rigot, A. (2022). If tech fails to design for the most vulnerable, it fails us all. *Wired.* https://www.wired.com/author/afsaneh-rigot/.

Tellis, G. J. (2013). *Unrelenting innovation: How to create a culture for market dominance.* Jossey-Bass.

Walsh, L. & Walker, K. C. (2016). Perspectives on uncertainty for technical communication scholars. *Technical Communication Quarterly, 24*(2), 71–86. http://dx.doi.org/10.10 80/10572252.2016.1150517.

West-Puckett, S. (2016). Making writing assessment more visible, equitable, and portable through digital badging. *College English, 79*(2), 123–147.

19. Human Factors and Ergonomics

Jack T. Labriola
TRUIST FINANCIAL CORPORATION

Definition and Background

The term *human factors and ergonomics* has had a long, rich history intertwined with the advent of more sophisticated tools and technologies. And while there are some debates about the true starting point to the field of human factors and ergonomics, one of the most influential moments in marking the importance of the field was World War II and the design of cockpits for fighter pilots. After an extensive study of over 460 "pilot error experiences" as fighter planes became more advanced, it was determined that there was an increased need to focus on the human (or pilot) and their physical and cognitive limitations for flying a plane and how a design should be developed with these limitations in mind (Fitts & Jones, 1947). From this point on, a former WWII lieutenant, Alphonse Chapanis, continued to work through this kind of research for the next several decades, even giving the keynote address at the 1988 conference for the Human Factors Association of Canada.

During this keynote address, Chapanis tackled the widening divide over usage of either human factors or ergonomics. He stated that "Whether we call ourselves human factors engineers or ergonomists is mostly an accident of where we happen to live and where we were trained" (qtd. in Chapanis, 1991, p. 2). Today, the International Ergonomics Association (2000) defines "Ergonomics (or human factors) [as] the scientific discipline concerned with the understanding of interactions among humans and other elements of a system, and the profession that applies theory, principles, data and methods to design in order to optimize human well-being and overall system performance." Building off of this definition, the Human Factors and Ergonomics Society (2019) adds that "Ergonomics and human factors use knowledge of human abilities and limitations to design systems, organizations, jobs, machines, tools, and consumer products for safe, efficient, and comfortable human use."

Design Application

A popular and current example of how human factors and ergonomics affects everyday life can be seen in the ways that chairs, desks, and computers are designed for their users. Some of these ergonomic design choices are developing, designing, and ***testing*** that go into the back support of a chair, the height of the desk, the height of a computer monitor, and the physical design of the keyboard that the user is working with in their work environment.

DOI: https://doi.org/10.37514/TPC-B.2022.1725.2.19

Human factors and ergonomics can be thought of as being closely related to the field of *usability* and user experience (UX). While some might think of user experience as focusing more on software, websites, and mobile app designs, human factors and ergonomics can be thought of as focusing more on the physical development of hardware or other physical devices and products that a user interacts with (UX Stack Exchange, 2014). For example, if we think of those with a background in usability or UX focusing on testing with users for navigational issues on a new car's digital touchscreen, someone with a background in human factors and ergonomics would additionally be testing whether or not the screen was big enough for the user to see/read from their sitting position, whether or not they could reach the buttons from their seat safely, and whether or not the mental workload of driving the car and operating the digital screen was viable.

In the end, both human factors/ergonomics and user experience focus primarily on bringing the user of a product or experience to the forefront of the research process, and they are both integral parts of creating an effective and safe product.

■ Pedagogical Integration

While courses in human factors and ergonomics are usually offered through human physiology, psychology, and occupational safety departments, technical communicators and designers are becoming increasingly invested in this domain from the perspective of *user-centered design*. Today, it is not uncommon to find interdisciplinary curricular initiatives in higher education where experts from across the previously mentioned disciplines collaborate to provide training to emerging technical communication professionals. Especially at a time when immersive media such as virtual reality, augmented reality, and mixed reality technologies are commonplace, technical communicators should equip themselves with knowledge of human sensation and perception to inform communication design.

Instructors may assign projects that allow students to learn how human physicality affects information retrieval, processing, and retention. Examples of learning activities include examining human-screen interaction through eye tracking, understanding human-information interaction through job analysis at specific sites through *contextual inquiry* (e.g., coffee shops, restaurants, libraries), exploring user experience through journey mapping (i.e., documenting the particular steps in completing a task), and studying physical and mental limitations in a physical space like a vehicle (even while parked).

An example assignment/activity to demonstrate the need for a human factors and ergonomics lens when conducting usability testing might look as follows:

1. Give a scenario in which students must design a brand new physical product such as a kitchen stove.

2. When the students are beginning to think about the design, functionality, and features of the new stove, ask them about things like the stove's size, dimensions, and placement of different buttons, knobs, and handles.

3. Ask students to try using their stove at their home(s) and to make note of any time something is hard to reach, press, or use either due to physical limitations (can't reach because they are too short/tall, hard to bend down, etc.) or mental limitations (cannot remember what something does).

4. Ask students to start to determine possible alternative design solutions based on human factors and how they would test for these things in their project(s).

In any of these learning activities, students should pay attention to human factors issues, processes or tools that contribute to the issues, and the potential ways to overcome those issues.

■ References and Recommended Readings

Chapanis, A. (1991). To communicate the human factors message, you have to know what the message is, and how to communicate it. *Human Factors Society Bulletin*, *34*(11), 1–6.

Fitts, P. M. & Jones, R. E. (1947). *Analysis of factors contributing to 460 "pilot error" experiences in operating aircraft controls* (Report No. TSEAA–694–12). Aero Medical Laboratory, Air Materiel Command, U.S. Air Force.

Human Factors and Ergonomics Society. (2019). *What is human factors/ergonomics?* https://www.hfes.org/about-hfes/what-is-human-factorsergonomics.

International Ergonomics Association. (2000). *Definition and domains of ergonomics.* https://iea.cc/what-is-ergonomics/.

Sanders, M. S. & McCormick, E. J. (1993). *Human factors in engineering and design* (7th ed.). McGraw Hill Inc.

Shaver, E. (2015, February 9). *Human Factors - A Brief History.* http://www.ericshaver.com/human-factors-a-brief-history/.

Usability Body of Knowledge. (2011, May). *Physical Ergonomics.* https://www.usability bok.org/physical-ergonomics.

UX Stack Exchange. (2014). *What is the difference between human factors and UX design?* https://ux.stackexchange.com/questions/69720/what-is-the-difference-between -human-factors-and-ux-design.

20. Inclusion

Zarah C. Moeggenberg
Metropolitan State University

Definition and Background

Inclusion is what it means to be considered and included within a group, design, or opportunity. It is most felt (or measured) when people know that their ideas and input are going to be leveraged in a given situation. In technical and professional communication (TPC), inclusion helps us to move beyond our own needs, desires, and goals for design and design thinking, and opens space to consider others who may benefit greatly from design thinking that engages their perspective. The social justice turn in technical communication has centralized inclusion in design thinking; yet, inclusion has been at the fore of user experience (UX) and design since the 1990s. As April O'Brien points out in her entry on *social justice* later in this collection, social justice issues, such as disability and accessibility (Colton & Walton, 2015; Hitt 2018; Melonçon, 2017), gender and sexuality (Cox, 2018a, 2018b; Edenfield, 2019), feminism (Frost & Haas, 2017; Moeller & Frost, 2016), and race (Williams & Pimentel, 2014) are strongly tied to inclusion. Of course, this list is in no way exhaustive.

While inclusion has been an ongoing part of TPC for some time, Natasha N. Jones, Kristen R. Moore, and Rebecca Walton (2016) have called for the field to create a more vivid antenarrative. They assert that "dominant narratives of efficiency, technological expertise, and innovative infrastructure too often dominate the field and research projects where inclusion sits at the heart of the project" (Jones et al., 2016, p. 213). As part of their ongoing efforts to create an antenarrative for TPC scholars, Jones et al. (2016) offer a heuristic for moving inclusion forward in the field, the 3Ps: positionality, power, and privilege. This situates us in thinking more critically about marginalization, disempowerment, and the promotion of agency and advocacy (Jones et al., 2016, p. 420).

In design thinking, we often associate the stage of *empathy*, or empathizing with the user, with inclusion, as it is key to generating "human-centered products and services" (Shalamova, 2016). Inclusion, however, can be critical to every stage of design thinking. Empathy, if anything, reminds us that design thinking should be participatory throughout. When we localize inclusion within social justice-driven work, we decentralize the role of the designer as the authority. In this collection's *participatory design* chapter, Ian Weaver emphasizes that we can challenge the notion of the designer as the expert by involving users in the full design process. Similarly, inclusion should not be thought of as a static practice or centered in one stage or moment within design thinking. Rather, inclusion is an

DOI: https://doi.org/10.37514/TPC-B.2022.1725.2.20

"active localization practice that includes whether or not diversity and difference is explicitly named and in what ways" (Shivers-McNair & San Diego, 2017). In other words, inclusion is a dynamic process whereby a practitioner, researcher, or designer critically examines positionality, power, and privilege through engaged listening, conversation, and participation with users.

■ Design Application

Let's consider some of the professional writing produced for communities by hospitals. Consider videos that appear on departmental profiles, like that of a postpartum depression informational video. Such a video is important because it not only defines postpartum depression, but it also lists symptoms one might look for postpartum. The video features a patient, a doctor, definition, symptom lists, and contact information. Within the design of both the webpage and the video itself are clear indications that inclusion was considered: written transcript, captions, an audio only file, and a link to a version in Spanish. These moves make the video accessible to people who are Deaf or Hard of Hearing (DHH), those who speak Spanish, and people with disabilities. But even while this may be a standard practice at a given hospital, it's important to reflect upon positionality, power, and privilege and ask, "How am I embodied—represented, manifested, or subjected—in this space as a designer?" as well as "Who is missing from this resource?"

Such questions about inclusion, especially in teams, help us to consider how inclusive the design of a text is. They might lead us to realize that only White users are shown and are occupying spaces in the video. Or, we might be led to include more statistics on postpartum depression and how this affects Black, Indigenous, and People of Color (BIPOC) at much higher rates. This may lead to follow-up with the physician featured in the video and scholarly research. And this all helps to create 1) a more inclusive resource for community members and 2) a reminder to do this with resources we create in the future.

■ Pedagogical Integration

A viable way to cultivate inclusivity is by modeling inclusive concepts and practices in the classroom. Of course, foregrounding these into assignments is critical. For example, if students are to produce a video, it should be scaffolded in that they create captions and/or a transcript. Likewise, if they're creating a webtext, it should be a standard expectation that images would have alt text for anyone accessing the site who uses a screen reader. These moves help to 1) cultivate an inclusive space where diverse experiences of texts are foregrounded into the design process and 2) open a channel for discussing difficult issues related to oppression and marginalization.

Regardless of the project students are working on, there are key questions that are useful to return to often when situating inclusion in the TPC students do together:

- How am I present in the design? How are my team members?
- How would I describe my own positionality and privilege relevant to the project?
- How did our values become embodied in the design?
- How can I embody the primary users more fully? What about tertiary users?
- How did users' values become embodied in the design?
- Who is missing? Or, who might have a hard time understanding, using, or applying what we are creating?
- What is my positionality, relevant to the stakeholders?
- How might that be affecting the design?

These questions provide a useful framework for continuously returning to inclusion throughout the design thinking process. The TPC classroom can also be a space where diversity and inclusion are celebrated, not just for namesake but with true intentions to promote underrepresented perspectives and experiences. In course readings and lesson examples, instructors should work to ensure representations of diverse perspectives and cultures. Students should be given the opportunities to grapple with difficult topics or conversations regarding differences based on their backgrounds, values, and beliefs. When designing solutions, students should be prompted to exercise inclusive practices so as to enact ideas and directions that reflect empathy, tolerance, and acceptance.

■ References and Recommended Readings

Colton, J. S. & Walton, R. (2015). Disability as insight into social justice pedagogy in technical communication. *Journal of Interactive Technology & Pedagogy, 8*. https://digitalcommons.usu.edu/english_facpub/731/.

Cox, M. (2018a). Shifting grounds as the new status quo: Examining queer theoretical approaches to diversity and taxonomy in the technical communication classroom. In A. M. Haas & M. F. Eble (Eds.), *Key theoretical frameworks: Teaching technical communication in the twenty-first century* (pp. 287–303). Utah State University Press.

Cox, M. (2018b). Working closets: Mapping queer professional discourses and why professional communication studies needs queer rhetorics. *Journal of Business and Technical Communication, 33*(1), 1–25. https://doi.org/10.1177/1050651918798691.

Edenfield, A. C., Holmes, S. & Colton, J. S. (2019). Queering tactical technical communication: DIY HRT. *Technical Communication Quarterly, 28*(3), 177–191, https://doi.org/10.1080/10572252.2019.1607906.

Frost, E. A. & Haas, A. M. (2017). Seeing and knowing the womb: A technofeminist reframing of fetal ultrasound toward a decolonization of our bodies. *Computers and Composition, 43*, 88–105. https://doi.org/10.1016/j.compcom.2016.11.00.4

Hitt, A. (2018). Foregrounding accessibility through (inclusive) design in professional communication curricula. *Business and Professional Communication Quarterly, 81*(1), 52–65.

Inclusive Design. (2018). Microsoft. https://www.microsoft.com/design/inclusive.

Jones, N. N. (2016). The technical communicator as advocate: Integrating a social justice approach in technical communication. *Journal of Technical Writing and Communication, 46*(3), 342–361. https://doi.org/10.1177/0047281616639472.

Jones, N. N., Moore, K. R. & Walton, R. (2016). Disrupting the past to disrupt the future: An antenarrative of technical communication. *Technical Communication Quarterly, 25*(4), 211–229. http://dx.doi.org/10.1080/10572252.2016.1224655.

Melonçon, L. (2017). *Rhetorical accessibility: At the intersection of technical communication and disability studies*. Routledge.

Moeller, M. E. & Frost, E. A. (2016). Food fights: Cookbook rhetorics, monolithic constructions of womanhood, and field narratives in technical communication. *Technical Communication Quarterly, 25*(1), 1–11.

Shalamova, N. (2016). Blending engineering content with design thinking and UX to maximize student engagement in a technical communication class. In *Proceedings of IEEE International Professional Communication Conference (IPCC)* (pp. 1–5). IEEE. https://doi.org/10.1109/IPCC.2016.7740493.

Shivers-McNair, A. & San Diego, C. (2017). Localizing communities, goals, communication and inclusion: A collaborative approach. *Technical Communication, 64*(2), 97–112.

Walton, R., Moore, K. R. & Jones, N. N. (2019). *Technical communication after the social justice turn: Building coalitions for action*. Routledge.

Williams, M. F. & Pimentel, O. (2014). *Communicating race, ethnicity, and identity in technical communication*. Baywood Publishing.

21. Innovation

Andrew Kulak
Triple Point Security & Virginia Tech

Definition and Background

Derived from a Latin verb meaning "changed" or "renewed," *innovation* is an intentional break from established practice that addresses a problem in a novel or unexpected way. As a process for finding creative solutions to *wicked problems*, design thinking is often presented as a replicable method to achieve innovative results. Innovation can be positive for individuals, communities, and the environment by increasing quality of life and improving efficiency, but there is also a more troubling sense of innovation that foregrounds rapid deployment of new technologies without considering individual lived experiences and communities. We should keep both senses in mind as we work to foster constructive design thinking and positive innovation.

A great example of positive innovation is the curb cut, or the little ramps built into curbs at intersections (99 Percent Invisible, 2021). Curb cuts address the challenge of sudden elevation changes in the built environment by breaking with traditional curb design through removing material from curbs to create gentle inclines at regular intervals that afford increased mobility. This design intervention supports disabled individuals as well as other people, such as those riding bikes, pushing strollers, or making deliveries using hand trucks. Curb cuts solve the real problems of a diverse community of users, and they do so not through the addition of some new technology but rather through the modification and maintenance of existing infrastructure (Chachra, 2015).

Products described as innovative, however, do not always share such positive qualities. Lately, innovation has become a buzzword, eliciting vague visions of new technologies and streamlined processes without accounting for the impact of technological changes on the lives of users (Zhexembayeva, 2020). Matthew Wisnioski (2015) argued that the sense of innovation primarily as delivery of a new and financially lucrative technology product arose in part from a cadre of industrialists, technologists, and policymakers who launched a networking organization called The Innovation Group in 1969. The group produced a magazine called *Innovation*, boasting a subscription price that placed it among the most expensive periodicals of the time, which "chronicled with gusto how a select few could achieve astonishing levels of creative and financial success" (qtd. in Wisnioski, 2015, p. 61). Targeted toward technologists, who were predominantly White and male, the magazine offered interviews and articles that painted a picture of the innovator as a man who leveraged social and technological change and

DOI: https://doi.org/10.37514/TPC-B.2022.1725.2.21

took creative risks to achieve financial success. This kind of innovation centers the development and marketing of new technology products, especially digital products that "disrupt" existing practices or even entire industries.

As a result, a tension exists between innovation as an outcome of creative and thoughtful design practice and innovation as a buzzword reflecting Silicon Valley cynicism, a tendency to "move fast and break things," driven by financial gain and a cursory (at best) consideration of how technologies actually impact people and communities (Taneja, 2019). We would do well to keep in mind that what counts as innovation always lies at the intersection of what is understood as a worthwhile problem to solve, what constitutes a valuable solution, and who derives value from a particular solution. These ethical and political dimensions of innovation should inform how we approach design. To foster positive innovation, we should adopt design frameworks that focus on people and communities and challenge assumptions about new technologies and marketability.

■ Design Implications

The design methods that we use are critical to developing an ethical and reflexive approach to innovation that seeks to realize changes to existing systems that will deliver real benefit to users. To address the assumptions inherent in any design process, design firms like IDEO (2015) champion human-centered design. Human-centered design is one approach to design thinking that seeks to address the ethical and political aspects of innovation by involving individuals and communities throughout the design process. Through methods that emphasize interaction with potential users, such as structured interviews, open conversations, and immersive participation in common activities, human-centered design establishes *empathy* as the cornerstone of an effective design process. By building empathy through research, designers can realize positive innovations that empower members of a community.

Similar to human-centered design, technical and professional communication research in *participatory design* suggests that innovative solutions should reflect social and cultural context and incorporate "the tacit knowledge developed and used by those who work with technologies" (Spinuzzi, 2005, p. 165). Participatory design reimagines design as research that combines the tacit knowledge of individuals and communities with the analytic and theoretical knowledge of experts through cooperative work. Here again, positive innovation emerges as the collaborative realization of shared community concerns, values, desires, and dreams.

Outside of such a critical and constructive approach, innovation quickly regresses toward technical gimmicks, where the term might describe something like the Juicero, the $400 juicer produced by a Silicon Valley startup that did little more than squeeze a juice box into a glass. Evgeny Morozov (2013) critiqued this kind of innovation as technological solutionism, which he defined as "an intellectual pathology that recognizes problems as problems based on just one criterion: whether they are 'solvable' with a nice and clean technological solution at our disposal." For Morozov, solutionism encompassed not only banal consumer products but also trite, one-off solutions to *wicked problems*, such as global warming, that fail to appreciate the social and technological complexity of these kinds of design challenges.

Human-centered design, participatory design, and related methods and methodologies help to avoid solutionism. These frameworks broaden design practice to include diverse individuals and stakeholders in order to help ensure that the value realized by a solution accrues to all members of a community. Using a process-based approach, designers seeking positive innovation form diverse cross-functional teams, brainstorm together, work with participants from relevant communities through *contextual inquiry*, complete *rapid prototypes* and *testing*, and practice *iteration* as they move through the different stages of their projects. In these moments, a design team can learn where the value lies in a given solution, who is included, and who is potentially left out. This design mindset can be developed in the technical and professional writing classroom.

■ Pedagogical Integration

To teach positive innovation strategies, instructors can assign problem-based, long-term group projects using a student-centered course structure. Projects should center on communities outside of the classroom rather than specific deliverables, and assignments should help students engage collaboratively with design thinking methods, ethical commitments, and community contexts. Early project phases should involve students working within their communities using *contextual inquiry* to build *empathy* with potential users. Rather than go into a project with a fixed idea of the solution, students should practice *problem definition* based on their insights from contextual research and use *rapid prototyping* and *testing* to validate that their solution works for users.

Problem-based projects that students address through design thinking and *iteration*, however, can be challenging to implement. Students will need appropriate scaffolding and daily activities as they determine potential communities to work with, identify relevant sites for contextual inquiry, and develop and test their solutions. This is a great opportunity to practice working in technical genres such as memos, proposals, and progress reports. But because work outside of the classroom is unpredictable, each phase of these projects also presents the possibility of failure.

Failing is common in design work. Embracing failure and understanding it as a learning opportunity can help us recognize areas where we do not completely understand the community where we are working and can lead us toward more productive solutions to consider. In the classroom, cultivating a mindset accepting of failure requires not only developing allowances in assessment but also contending with a broader academic culture where failure is simply not tolerated.

Accommodating failure requires flexibility so that students who put a great deal of effort into a project that does not work out are not penalized. For example, this could include modifying assignment sequences if a research site falls through or changing a deliverable from a report to a reflective "postmortem" for a prototype evaluation session that did not go as planned. In addition, emphasizing the design process rather than specific products can be beneficial given that products may not work out and may need to be changed during a real-world design project.

Practices to document the design process include writing or drawing on Post-it notes during *ideation*, affinity diagramming, wireframing, ***rapid prototyping***, and the Visible Thinking Tools developed by Harvard's Project Zero (2017). Working in different modalities, such as handwriting rather than typing, sketching, or creating 3D models, can help to promote different ways of approaching a given topic while at the same time generating design thinking artifacts that trace the history of a project. Journaling throughout the design process helps to surface insights that may otherwise be forgotten and to consolidate new information. All of these resources can also be used to gain insight into a design group's work and overall progress (and factored into assessment).

Taken together, practices focused on process not only support pragmatic considerations like documentation and assessment but also encourage regular collaboration, introspection, and reflection. Throughout their design work and reflections, students can practice design methods, develop their own design thinking process, and build a human-centered theory of innovation.

■ References and Recommended Readings

99 Percent Invisible (2021, April 27). *Curb cuts*. https://99percentinvisible.org/episode/curb-cuts/.

Bazerman, C. (2002). *The languages of Edison's light*. MIT Press.

Chachra, D. (2015, January 23). Why I am not a maker. *The Atlantic*. https://www.theatlantic.com/technology/archive/2015/01/why-i-am-not-a-maker/384767.

Feldman, M. P. (2013). *The geography of innovation*. Springer Science & Business Media.

Gertner, J. (2013). The idea factory: Bell Labs and the great age of American innovation. Penguin.

IDEO. (2015). *The field guide to human-centered design*. http://www.designkit.org/resources/1.

MacKay, W. E. (1999). Is paper safer? The role of paper flight strips in air traffic control. *ACM Transactions on Computer-Human Interaction, 6*(4), 311–340.

McBride, A. M. & Mlyn, E. (2015, February 2). Innovation alone won't fix social problems. *The Chronicle of Higher Education*. https://www.chronicle.com/article/Innovation-Alone-Won-t-Fix/151551.

Morozov, E. (2013). *To save everything, click here: The folly of technological solutionism*. PublicAffairs.

Nielsen, J. (2009, February 1). *Macintosh: 25 years*. Nielsen Norman Group. https://www.nngroup.com/articles/macintosh-25-years/.

Project Zero. (2017). *Visible thinking tools*. Harvard Graduate School of Education. https://pz.harvard.edu/resources/visible-thinking-tools.

Selfe, C. L. & Selfe, R. J. (1994). The politics of the interface: Power and its exercise in electronic contact zones. *College Composition and Communication, 45*(4), 480–504.

Spinuzzi, C. (2005). The methodology of participatory design. *Technical Communication, 52*(2), 163–175.

Taneja, H. (2019, January 22). The era of "move fast and break things" is over. *Harvard Business Review*. https://hbr.org/2019/01/the-era-of-move-fast-and-break-things -is-over .

Thompson, D. (2017). Google X and the science of radical creativity. *The Atlantic*. https://www.theatlantic.com/magazine/archive/2017/11/x-google-moonshot-factory/540648/.

Todhunter, J. (2009, April 22). Defining innovation. *Fast Company*. https://www.fastcompany.com/1273187/defining-innovation.

Vinsel, L. (2015, November 12). *95 theses on innovation*. http://leevinsel.com/blog/2015/11/12/95-theses-on-innovation.

Wisnioski, M. (2015). The birth of innovation. *IEEE Spectrum, 52*(2), 40–61. https://doi.org/10.1109/MSPEC.2015.7024510.

Zhexembayeva, N. (2020, February 19). Stop calling it "innovation." *Harvard Business Review*. https://hbr.org/2020/02/stop-calling-it-innovation.

22. Modularity

Adam Strantz
MIAMI UNIVERSITY

Definition and Background

As a concept in design thinking, modularity is a useful way to segment out the design process into more manageable tasks. Carliss Y. Baldwin and Kim B. Clark (2000) define modularity as an approach where "different parts of the computer could be designed by separate, specialized groups working independently of one another. The 'modules' could then be connected and (in theory at least) would function seamlessly, as long as they conformed to a predetermined set of design rules" (p. 6). Beyond this approach to computer design, Ellen Lupton and Jennifer Cole Phillips (2015) use the concept of modularity in design by defining modules as any "fixed element within a larger system" that can be readily applied to many design thinking problems. So, modules may be interchangeable parts of a computer system, or required design parameters such as those defined by a company's style guide. Just as the engineer can slot different modular pieces of a computer together to quickly build a system, the designer can take elements such as the client's logo or color scheme and prototype a design around those fixed elements. Modules can also be any items or tasks separated out to different individuals working on a singular project—for example, separating out written content, layout, images, and media from a website design. The key is the separate-yet-connected nature of the modules and the ability for designers to work on modules individually and plug them together. By following modular practices, designers have room for experimentation, *iteration*, and *innovation* by clearly defining what parts of the design are fixed modules and then focusing their attention on the more fluid elements of the design process.

Joel Sadler et al. (2016) use modularity as a way to enhance *rapid prototyping* in the design thinking process. They write, "A component with a high degree of modularity has fewer dependencies on outside variables. In prototyping, this implies that modules enable designers to freely try combinations of parts, much like adding bricks in a toy construction kit" (Sadler et al., 2016, pp. 142–143). Designers are therefore able to use modular components to quickly build prototypes or proof-of-concept models and experiment with the design by taking apart and combining elements. Although the modules provide some constraints in the design process, they conversely aid in experimentation by allowing the designer to try out various ideas more quickly by prototyping around these fixed elements. As an example, modern web design has increasingly moved toward a modular, component-based design model. Popular web design frameworks such

DOI: https://doi.org/10.37514/TPC-B.2022.1725.2.22

as Bootstrap, React, Angular, and Google's Material Design rely on modular components that can be quickly combined to create a functioning website or application instead of coding everything from scratch. The design can then be quickly populated with content in order to secure funding, provide a working model for user testing, or experiment with additional features.

Design Application

Modularity is an emerging trend due to its potential benefits in cost reduction brought about by the functional partitioning of a designed system or solution. Modular design has also influenced technical communication by promoting modular documentation. As single-source writing and dynamic content delivery become increasingly commonplace in industry, technical communicators are creating and reusing modular content to ensure sustainability and efficiency for content as it moves across contexts or formats. For example, communicators may use modular documentation in the ideation and prototyping phases of the design thinking process to quickly build out sections of text or design elements that will be standardized across a number of documents/designs. These modular pieces of content can further help ensure consistency as the content is used in multiple formats such as print/digital as well as shared across teams or working groups in the company.

In essence, modular documentation begins with understanding content requirements and defining content construction and maintenance strategy. Once these steps are done, technical communicators develop content modules (units of content) in chunks, such as a description, an overview, a task, a step, etc. These modules, like LEGO blocks, can be pieced together in different ways for different purposes, hence increasing efficiency and reducing cost of production since the modules can be reused and updated individually. Modern information mapping and development models like the DITA (Darwin Information Typing Architecture) standards and design systems such as those used for web frameworks like Bootstrap, Angular, or React are examples of modular writing in technical communication that students may use in the workplace.

Pedagogical Integration

For students learning the design thinking process, modularity can prove to be a useful part of early prototyping and as an aspect of using constraints to inspire design. Ellen Lupton and Jennifer Cole Phillips (2015) helpfully define modules in a broad sense as any fixed element within a larger system that can be readily applied to many design thinking problems. Stemming from work on LEGO Serious Play (LEGO, 2019), where LEGO bricks are used as a team-building, hands-on learning device, LEGO can also be used as an activity for demonstrating modularity in the design thinking process. Thinking of the LEGO bricks themselves as individual modules that cannot be broken apart, students are encouraged to try different configurations, experiment, and *play* at design in a hands-on activity using materials that most of them are familiar with.

Starting with a quick introduction to building with LEGO and the combinations possible using the most basic of elements, six 2x4 red bricks (915,103,765 to be exact; Huw, 2017), students are split into teams and given a small bag of random LEGO bricks. The bag should contain elements such as wheels, wings, and plenty of small LEGO bricks that can be useful in a variety of builds. Students are then tasked with creating a vehicle or model using exactly half of the bricks. After finishing the first task, students trade their models with another group that must then "complete" the model by adding elements without removing any existing parts. Students are able to trade leftover elements with other groups as well as talk with the group they received the model from to help interpret what the model is supposed to be. Here, modularity and creativity are tested by working first from individual modules (the bricks themselves) up to larger constraints (the first model). The activity can also be further connected to other in-class activities, such as document design practice working from a style guide or design system where students have set parameters they cannot modify while still creating a unique product. In both the LEGO and document design activities, the key is to highlight the useful nature of modular design to speed up the design process while allowing for experimentation in working with other groups or playing with non-fixed elements.

■ References and Recommended Readings

Baldwin C. & Clark, K. (2000). *Design rules, Vol. 1: The power of modularity*. MIT Press.

Curtis, N. A. (2009). *Modular web design: Creating reusable components for user experience design and documentation*. Peachpit Press.

Huw. (2017). *Review: 624210 LEGO House 6 Bricks*. Brickset. https://brickset.com/article/30827/review-624210-lego-house-6-bricks.

LEGO Serious Play. (2019). LEGO. https://www.lego.com/en-us/seriousplay.

Lupton, E. & Phillips, J. C. (2015). *Graphic design: The new basics*. Princeton Architectural Press.

Sadler, J., Shluzas, L., Blikstein, P. & Katila, R. (2016). Building blocks of the maker movement: Modularity enhances creative confidence during prototyping. In H. Plattner, C. Meinel & L. Leifer (Eds.), *Design thinking research. Understanding innovation* (pp. 141–154). Springer; Cham.

23. Participatory Design

Ian R. Weaver
University of North Carolina Wilmington

Definition and Background

Participatory design engages users as full participants in each phase of the design process. It joins human- and *user-centered design* in prioritizing users' design input, but it first and foremost "raises questions of democracy, power, and control" (Ehn, 1992, p. 41), seeking to equalize power between designers and users by ensuring users become co-creators, not simply informants (e.g., Sanders & Stappers, 2008). The methodology originates from Scandinavian researchers' response to industrial power struggles. In the 1970s, researchers like Kristen Nygaard (e.g., Nygaard & Bergo, 1975) and the Norwegian and the Iron and Metal Workers Union project pioneered the methodology under the concept of "cooperative design" (Sundblad, 2010), in which trade unions collaborated with workers to influence how technologies were implemented in workplaces. The goal was to "engage workers in designing systems that would enhance rather than eliminate their jobs" (Simmons, 2007, p. 109). Participatory design has since been employed under varying terms—"codesign" and "cocreation" (Sanders & Stappers, 2008)—and related methodologies—community-based participatory research and participatory action research (The Denizen Designer Project, 2022).

Participatory design (PD) aims to position users as indispensable experts in creating and implementing—not merely improving the usability of—workplace technologies. From its inception, PD "has always given primacy to human action and people's rights to participate in the shaping of the worlds in which they act" (Simonsen & Robertson, 2012, p. 4). Holding to this intent, technical communication researchers and designers have applied PD beyond the workplace, including users as participants in design work such as community building and health literacy technologies (Green, 2020), health insurance guidebooks (Rose et al., 2017), environmental policy making (Simmons, 2007), neighborhood revitalization (Silverman et al., 2008), and urban and transportation planning (Moore, 2016; Moore & Elliott, 2016). Participatory design is an important methodology for design thinkers seeking to do community-based and participatory design work.

Common methods and techniques used and studied by technical communicators include usability studies with think-aloud protocols and task-based tests (Rose et al., 2017); narrative-based user experience (UX) interviews (Green, 2020); design ethnographies with rich descriptions, ride-alongs, and video diaries (Rose, 2016); focus groups, journaling, and surveys (Rea et al., 2018); gameplay (Thominet, 2021); and participant observations (Moore & Elliot, 2016).

■ Design Application

Two primary values guide applying design thinking with a PD framework: 1) incorporating users' tacit knowledge into the design process and 2) building a democratic community through genuine participation (Björgvinsson et al., 2012). Technical communicators assume users have tacit knowledge—"know-how"—a type of implicit knowledge "about how a product will be used" that designers lack (Simmons, 2007, p. 109). Involving participants as doers and creators in design activities therefore becomes imperative in PD. In application, designers strive to make participant expertise discernible, visibly or through a sense of shared ownership. For example, Monique Janneck et al. (2006) sought to integrate free-lance IT and consulting professionals' knowledge into new management software. To do so, the designers used activities such as workshops, interviews, and focus groups as well as techniques like brainstorming and creating use scenarios to engage participants. Over an 18-month period, and through such "ongoing dialogue," the IT and consulting professionals came to regard the new software as "their development instead" of the designers' (Janneck et al., 2006, p. 276). Ownership was shared, and the users' expertise became visible.

The second guiding value is genuine participation (Simonsen & Robertson, 2012), which can be paired with building inclusive and democratic communities. Technical communicators have applied PD as a community-building methodology in *social justice* work. Joining other decolonial methodologies, such as Godwin Agboka's (2013) participatory localization, PD unites with "resource-weak" (Björgvinsson et al., 2012) participants to co-create knowledge and honor community practice. One such example comes from Mckinley Green's (2020) work to include end users in the design of an HIV youth outreach and education program. Using narrative-based UX interviews, Green observed community members resisting the program's deficit-based communication assumptions. The community members' participation through resistance "opened possibilities to redirect the organizational strategy toward empowerment and community building as frame-works for promoting equitable health outcomes" (Green, 2020, p. 11). Seeking genuine participation among community members, PD can help reshape contexts (like health literacy) defined by marginalization and oppression.

Seeking genuine participation is not without its problems, however. Andrea Cornwall (2008) censures designers' feigned democratic attempts and warns that applying a participatory approach does not guarantee socially just outcomes. Scholars like Luke Thominet (2020) also warn against standardizing "genuine participation" as doing so may overlook other forms of legitimate participation "not limited to events or processes created by the designer" (p. 362). Others point to the important difference between representative and full participation (e.g., Rose et al., 2017). Technical communication scholars have therefore produced heuristics (e.g., Simmons, 2007; Spinuzzi, 2005; Thominet, 2020) for assessing participation and altering PD practices to meet local needs, such as

Lisa Melonçon's (2017) patient experience design. Some guiding principles of genuine participation include ensuring users become decision makers, prioritizing mutual learning between users and designers, involving if not all then at least representative users, and making sure users participate in each stage of the design process.

Pedagogical Integration

In the classroom, PD can help students apply design ethics, cultivate empathy, and exercise inclusive design. Key questions for students to consider when designing a PD project include the following:

- Who is or will be impacted by the design?
- Who should we include?
- When, for how long, and in what ways should we involve participants?

Students may learn to facilitate PD by practicing ways to engage users, perform observations, and collect data. Key methods to introduce include contextual inquiry, ethnography, card sorting, product reaction cards, and focus group interviews (Rose, 2016). Students may be assigned into teams to create a mock PD session where they collaboratively devise a goal and plan (recruitment, logistics, agenda items) for the session, create prompts and instructions for participants, and run the session with classmates acting as participants (Rea et al., 2018).

After the students practice such activities, the instructor may help them reflect on the process and outcomes of the PD session, identifying ways to improve. Considering the project's purpose, context, and the chosen research vs. design activities can encourage conversations about why certain methods were selected and how such methods might be applied in future projects (Bratteteig et al., 2013). Dividing methods and techniques into classifications such as "say, do, make" activities may help students reflect on ways they can involve participants and for what purposes one method/technique is chosen over another (Sanders & Stappers, 2018; see also Brandt et al., 2013). It also might help to reflect on the limitations of PD, such as the required time and resources needed (Spinuzzi, 2005). Scholarship for such critique can include the conversations on "distributed PD" (e.g., Danielsson et al., 2009).

References and Recommended Readings

Agboka, G. Y. (2013). Participatory localization: A social justice approach to navigating unenfranchised/disenfranchised cultural sites. *Technical Communication Quarterly*, *22*(1), 28–49. https://doi.org/10.1080/10572252.2013.730966.

Bjögvinsson, E., Ehn, P. & Hillgren, P. A. (2012). Design things and design thinking: Contemporary participatory design challenges. *Design Issues*, *28*(3), 101–116. https://doi.org/10.1162/DESI_a_00165.

Brandt, E., Binder, T. & Sanders, E. B.-N. (2013). Tools and techniques: Ways to engage telling, making and enacting. In J. Simonsen & T. Robertson (Eds.), *Routledge international handbook of participatory design* (pp. 145–181). Routledge.

Bratteteig, T., Bødker, K., Dittrich, Y., Mogensen, P. H. & Simonsen, J. (2013). Methods: Organising principles and general guidelines for participatory design projects. In J. Simonsen & T. Robertson (Eds.), *Routledge international handbook of participatory design* (pp. 117–144). Routledge.

Cornwall, A. (2008). Unpacking "Participation": Models, meanings and practices. *Community Development Journal, 43*(3), 269–283.

Crawford, K. (2009). Following you: Disciplines of listening in social media. *Continuum, 23*(4), 525–535. http://doi.org/10.1080/10304310903003270.

Danielsson, K., Gumm, D. & Naghsh, A. M. (2009). Distributed PD: Challenges and opportunities. *Scandinavian Journal of Information Systems, 21*(1), 23–26.

Ehn, P. (1992). Scandinavian design: On participation and skill. In P. Adler & T. Winograd (Eds.), *Usability: Turning technologies into tools* (pp. 96–132). Oxford University Press.

Green, M. (2020). Resistance as participation: Queer theory's applications for HIV health technology design. *Technical Communication Quarterly, 30*(4), 331–344. https://doi.org/10.1080/10572252.2020.1831615.

Janneck, M., Finck, M. & Obendorf, H. (2006). Participatory Design: An issue for web-based community development?! In *Web Based Communities 2006: Proceedings of the IADIS International Conference Web Based Communities* (pp. 274–277).

Melonçon, L. K. (2017). Patient experience design: Expanding usability methodologies for healthcare. *Communication Design Quarterly Review, 5*(2), 19–28.

Moore, K. R. (2016). Public engagement in environmental impact studies: A case study of professional communication in transportation planning. *IEEE Transactions on Professional Communication, 59*(3), 245–260.

Moore, K. R. & Elliott, T. J. (2016). From participatory design to a listening infrastructure: A case of urban planning and participation. *Journal of Business and Technical Communication, 30*(1), 59–84. http://doi.org/10.1177/1050651915602294.

Nygaard, K. & Bergo, O. T. (1975). The Trade Unions-New users of research. *Personnel Review, 4*(2), 5–10.

Rea, J. M., Cannon, P., Sawchyn, A. & Walkup, K. L. (2018). Journaling and bibliotherapy participatory design as a heuristic for program development. In G. Y. Agboka & N. Matveeva (Eds.), *Citizenship and advocacy in technical communication* (pp. 153–174). Routledge.

Rose, E. J. (2016). Design as advocacy: Using a human-centered approach to investigate the needs of vulnerable populations. *Journal of Technical Writing and Communication, 46*(4), 427–445.

Rose, E. J., Racadio, R., Wong, K., Nguyen, S., Kim, J. & Zahler, A. (2017). Community-based user experience: Evaluating the usability of health insurance information with immigrant patients. *IEEE Transactions on Professional Communication, 60*(2), 214–231.

Sanders, E. B.-N. & Stappers, P. J. (2008). Co-creation and the new landscapes of design. *CoDesign, 4*(1), 5–18. http://doi.org/10.1080/15710880701875068.

Silverman, R. M., Taylor, H. L. & Crawford, C. (2008). The role of citizen participation and action research principles in Main Street revitalization: An analysis of a local planning project. *Action Research, 6*(1), 69–93. http://doi.org/10.1177/1476750307083725.

Simmons, M. W. (2007). *Participation and power: Civic discourse in environmental policy decisions.* SUNY Press.

Simonsen, J. & Robertson, T. (Eds.). (2012). *Routledge international handbook of participatory design.* Routledge.

Spinuzzi, C. (2005). The methodology of participatory design. *Technical Communication, 52*(2), 163–174. https://repositories.lib.utexas.edu/bitstream/handle/2152/28277/SpinuzziTheMethodologyOfParticipatoryDesign.pdf.

Sundblad, Y. (2010). UTOPIA: Participatory design from Scandinavia to the world. In *IFIP Conference on History of Nordic Computing* (pp. 176–186). Springer.

The Denizen Designer Project. (2022). *The Denizen Designer Project Report.* http://www.thedenizendesignerproject.com/denizendesigner/report.

Thominet, L. (2021). Open video game development and participatory design. *Technical Communication Quarterly, 30*(4), 359–374. https://doi.org/10.1080/10572252.2020.1866679.

24. Social Design

Liz Lane
University of Memphis

Definition and Background

What do we aim to accomplish when we design something? Who do we aim to reach? What is the broader purpose of design? These general questions are an entry point to social design, the notion that people, communities, and their needs should be central to all design decisions to "help promote positive change within society" (Resnick, 2016). Originally connected to the graphic and industrial design fields, social design, or design for social impact, has become more prominent in discussions about design thinking and designing with social justice issues in mind (see Rachael Sullivan's entry on *design ethics* and April O'Brien's entry on *social justice*, for example). At its core, social design challenges the designer to approach design scenarios as a means to "combat social issues" (Shea, 2012). Whether one is designing a public service advertisement for a bus stop or eco-conscious packaging for a consumer product, social design focuses on informing, persuading, and inspiring action toward social good in local and global communities. Social design centers the communal, the people-centric at all junctures of the design process, from its outset, iteration, to conclusion. A natural complement to *usability* and *user-centered design*, framing design scenarios through a social design approach values the user and their lived experience at the center of a design problem.

Social design is a critical thinking approach to help one frame collective design situations where something must be designed and communicated toward a specific, communal end goal. In reflecting on typical graphic design training and persuasive approaches, Victor Margolin (2011/2016) states that "expertise in persuading consumers to purchase products has become highly developed, now persuasion must be applied to promoting positive social behavior such as ethnic and racial tolerance, energy conservation, and overall environmental citizenship" (p. 15). Akin to design schemas such as design thinking that prioritize collaboration, empathy, and audience-centric deliverables, social design encourages industry practitioners, educators, and students to explore designing for those at the margins in order to better reach audiences most impacted by design, be it the design of a public park bench or the design of an immigration and border patrol informational brochure. In *Developing Citizen Designers*, a text of case studies of social design applied in varied settings, Elizabeth Resnick (2016) raises many of the questions that perplex practitioners and scholars in the fields of technical and professional communication or science and technology studies. Resnick wonders

DOI: https://doi.org/10.37514/TPC-B.2022.1725.2.24

how to help students, colleagues, and clients alike see the applicability and transferability of their work to their communities, arguing that "designers have both a social and a moral responsibility to use their visual language training to address societal issues either within or in addition to their professional design practice" (p. 12). "Designers" here can mean many pursuits: teachers, writers, graphic artists, engineers, and virtually any occupation that creates deliverables for public consumption or use.

■ Design Application

A strong case of social design in action is that of environmentally focused consumer brands, such as American clothing company Everlane. The company uses biodegradable packaging materials printed with statistics about a garment's material composition, including information about carbon expenditures behind each item produced and human labor hours invested in making each of their garments. This social design approach to their product packaging informs consumers about the material costs behind the goods they are purchasing (and wearing) while persuading their customers to learn more about labor production costs to the planet overall. Such transparent practices show social design working as a type of "design justice" that spotlights power structures and inequalities embedded in broader design contexts (Costanza-Chock, 2018). Social design is therefore an actionable critical thinking tool to use in concert with other design heuristics, continually urging one to spotlight the material impacts of design decisions and how to inspire change through design.

■ Pedagogical Integration

Students may learn to engage in social design as a way to aspire positive social change. A strategic way to integrate social design in a technical communication classroom is through community partnerships and open classroom discussion of power structures and societal issues in local communities. In consultation with the community partner (e.g., local businesses, federal agencies, or nonprofit organizations), the instructor may incorporate social design assignments that align with the learning objectives of the course. In a document design course, for instance, students may create visual or interactive documents that make design injustices more apparent (such as infographics or webtexts highlighting social design issues) for instructional or educational use by the partner organization. Using social design in the assignment, the students and instructor would carefully research and analyze the audiences most impacted by the documents (for example, underserved neighborhoods or specific demographic groups) and offer actions for readers/viewers to take. It is important to remember that the outcome of social design is more than just creating transparent communication materials; it is a deliberate effort to affect change through design and inspire action.

To ensure students have the opportunity to grapple with social issues, the instructor should coach them in ways to inquire information from participating community partners, audiences, and other stakeholders, and synthesize the critical impact of the identified issues in these groups' respective situations. Students may investigate the power and decision-making structures in their partner organization in order to understand the sources of authority and legitimacy or analyze the targeted audience of the project, carefully considering their positionality and needs. As a learning exercise, students may use these findings to fabricate a design solution to the specified social issue. The design project should conclude with a collective reflection by the students and community partners to assess the impact of their work.

■ References and Recommended Readings

Berman, D. B. (2008). *Do good design: How design can change our world.* Peachpit Press.

Costanza-Chock, S. (2018). Design justice: Towards an intersectional feminist framework for design theory and practice. In *Proceedings of the Design Research Society.* https://papers.ssrn.com/sol3/papers.cfm?abstract_id=3189696.

Costanza-Chock, S. (2020). *Design justice: Community-led practices to build the worlds we need.* MIT Press.

Margolin, V. (2016). Graphic design education and the challenge of social transformation. In E. Resnick (Ed.), *Developing citizen designers* (pp. 14–15). Bloomsbury. (Original work published 2011)

Resnick, E. (Ed.). (2016). *Developing citizen designers.* Bloomsbury.

Shea, A. (2012). *Designing for social change: Strategies for community-based graphic design.* Princeton Architectural Press.

25. Social Justice

April L. O'Brien
Sam Houston State University

Definition and Background

While technical communication has traditionally been regarded as an objective, unbiased, fact-driven field, over the last couple of decades, the field has experienced a movement towards cultural studies (Scott, 2003; Scott & Longo, 2006) as well as what Angela Haas and Michelle Eble (2018) call the "social justice turn." Social justice, as it is theorized and practiced in technical communication, is a large-scale amending of social injustice that affects humans, nonhuman animals, and the environment. To apply social justice frameworks to technical communication includes incorporating scholarship in cultural rhetorics, human rights and human dignity, feminism and gender studies, disability studies, race and ethnicity, intercultural communication, and community engagement. Although conversations in these research areas have been ongoing, the advancement to include them within the field of technical communication is relatively new and growing in momentum, as evidenced in recent and forthcoming publications (Agboka, 2012; Colton & Holmes, 2018; Haas, 2012; Jones et al., 2016; Shelton, 2020; Walton, 2016; Walton et al., 2019).

The social justice turn resulted from scholars openly acknowledging the need for inclusivity, as well as the need for scholars and practitioners to investigate how social and ideological identity markers impact the way we communicate. Instead of viewing these identity markers as isolated from the technical communication documents that we produce, this turn has brought theories and methods into conversation with each other. For example, social justice research argues that all technical communication situations are intercultural and that technical communicators must examine the role of systems of power (Agboka, 2012; Haas & Eble, 2018). As technical communicators consider relationships of power, some have studied the implications of environmental justice within minoritized communities in Dearborn, Michigan (Sackey, 2018), as well as how to communicate about climate change within multidisciplinary contexts (Cagle & Tillery, 2015). Social justice has informed the way technical communicators consider identity markers such as race, ethnicity, socio-economic status, country of origin, sexuality and gender, and ableness, and in doing so, interrogates seemingly objective documents to promote equity and transparency. While social justice concerns intersect with almost all conversations in technical communication, a few keywords in this collection are particularly relevant and informative when practiced alongside social justice principles. In this collection, Zarah C. Moeggenberg identifies the

DOI: https://doi.org/10.37514/TPC-B.2022.1725.2.25

field's interest in *inclusion* as a direct effect of the social justice turn. Likewise, Rachael Sullivan addresses the importance of ***design ethics*** to account for a variety of social justice contexts, and Ashanka Kumari examines how the application of ***equity*** promotes a design environment that accounts for all bodies.

■ Design Application

In terms of design thinking, integrating social justice contexts has changed the way the field studies and creates. For example, software engineers have examined how code and coding are inherently biased and how computer algorithms exhibit the racist and/or sexist leanings of their designers. In terms of user experience (UX), technical communication is more concerned about the accessibility of design and considering which bodies are not able to access certain projects. Another perspective is human-centered design (HCD), which is a way that technical communicators have sought to design documents that are more equitable and just (Friess, 2010; Jones & Wheeler, 2016; Walton, 2016). This kind of design places people at the center of projects and works to empower users, regardless of their race, class, gender, sexuality, country of origin, or ableness.

Langdon Winner's (1986) study of architect Robert Moses' designs presents an excellent example of what happens when social justice is not incorporated into design principles. Moses, who was responsible for countless park, road, and bridge designs in the first half of the 20th century, is infamous for designing a low-clearance overpass in Long Island that prevented buses from accessing many parkways, as well as Jones Beach. This design was intentionally biased to prevent impoverished residents, as well as Black and Brown people, from moving about these spaces and places (Haas, 2012; Sackey, 2018; Slack & Wise, 2005). This illustration underscores the significance of social justice matters within making and design. While there is much more work to be done to revamp making and design thinking within a social justice framework, the field of technical communication has made significant strides over the last several years.

■ Pedagogical Integration

There is a growing community and body of knowledge that support integrations of social justice activism in our pedagogy. For example, the Digital Rhetoric Collaborative out of the University of Michigan Sweetland Center for Writing has curated a wiki resource for teaching social justice in the technical communication classroom ("Social justice," 2017). The case example on the wiki shared the conclusion that social justice is not optional to technical communication, and thus students must engage with advocacy work that resonates with their values and beliefs. A viable assignment that introduces this importance involves having students examine an everyday technology (e.g., microwave, Keurig coffee maker, Fitbit tracker, Apple iPad) and its associated technical communication (e.g., user guide, help documentation, customer support resources). Students can be assigned to perform a socio-rhetorical analysis to understand the intersection of ideologies and issues of class, race, gender, and ability in the design and use of technical tools and documents.

■ References and Recommended Readings

Agboka, G. (2012). Liberating intercultural technical communication from "large culture" ideologies: Constructing culture discursively. *Journal of Technical Writing and Communication, 42*(2), 159–181.

Cagle, L. E. & Tillery, D. (2015). Climate change research across disciplines: The value and uses of multidisciplinary research reviews for technical communication. *Technical Communication Quarterly, 24*(2), 147–163.

Colton, J. S. & Holmes, S. (2018). A social justice theory of active equality for technical communication. *Journal of Technical Writing and Communication, 48*(1), 4–30.

Friess, E. (2010). The sword of data: Does human-centered design fulfill its rhetorical responsibility? *Design Issues, 26*(3), 40–50.

Haas, A. M. (2012). Race, rhetoric, and technology: A case study of decolonial technical communication theory, methodology, and pedagogy. *Journal of Business and Technical Communication, 26*(3), 277–310.

Haas, A. M. & Eble, M. F. (Eds.). (2018). *Key theoretical frameworks: Teaching technical communication in the twenty-first century.* Utah State University Press.

Jones, N. N., Moore, K. R. & Walton, R. (2016). Disrupting the past to disrupt the future: An antenarrative of technical communication. *Technical Communication Quarterly, 25*(4), 211–229.

Jones, N. N. & Wheeler, S. K. (2016). Document design and social justice: A universal design for documents. In E. Wardle & D. Downs (Eds.), *Writing about writing: A college reader* (pp. 654–673). Bedford/St. Martin's.

Jones, N. N. & Williams, M. F. (2018). Technologies of disenfranchisement: Literacy tests and Black voters in the US from 1890 to 1965. *Technical Communication, 65*(4). https://www.stc.org/techcomm/2018/11/08/technologies-of-disenfranchisement-literacy-tests-and-black-voters-in-the-us-from–1890-to–1965/.

Sackey, D. J. (2018). An environmental justice paradigm for technical communication. In A. M. Haas & M. F. Eble (Eds.), *Key theoretical frameworks: Teaching technical communication in the twenty-first century* (pp. 138–160). Utah State University Press.

Scott, J. B. (2003). *Risky rhetoric: AIDS and the cultural practices of HIV testing.* Southern Illinois University Press.

Scott, J. B. & Longo, B. (Eds.). (2006). Guest editors' introduction: Making the cultural turn. *Technical Communication Quarterly, 15*(1), 3–7.

Shelton, C. (2020). Shifting out of neutral: Centering difference, bias, and social justice in a Business Writing course. *Technical Communication Quarterly, 29*(1), 18–32.

Slack, J. D. & Wise, J. M. (2005). *Culture + technology: A primer.* Lang.

Social justice through technical communication: Teaching resources. (2017). In *Digital Rhetoric Collaborative.* http://webservices.itcs.umich.edu/mediawiki/DigitalRhetoric Collaborative/index.php/Social_Justice_though_Technical_Communication: _Teaching_Resources.

Walton, R. (2016). Supporting human dignity and human rights: A call to adopt the first principle of human-centered design. *Journal of Technical Writing and Communication, 46*(4), 402–426.

Walton, R., Moore, K. R. & Jones, N. N. (2019). *Technical communication after the social justice turn.* Routledge.

Winner, L. (1986). Do artifacts have politics? In L. Winner (Ed.), *The whale and the reactor: A search for limits in an age of high technology* (pp. 19–39). University of Chicago Press.

26. Tacit Knowledge

Kristen R. Moore
UNIVERSITY AT BUFFALO

Definition and Background

Tacit knowledge might best be defined as knowledge that lives in action or in doing, defying the objective measures of empirical study (Moore & Elliott, 2016). Know-how (tacit) knowledge is created, maintained, and transferred differently than know-what (explicit) knowledge, challenging designers, communicators, and managers alike to capture and understand the role of tacit knowledge in design processes and organizational development (cf. Durá et al., 2019; Spinuzzi, 2002, 2005). Because tacit knowledge is often unspoken—if not unspeakable—designers involve users in nontraditional forms of explanation like demonstration, use, and performance. Explaining how to ride a bike is easier if you perform or demonstrate your know-how than if you rely on words alone.

Researchers in design thinking take particular interest in tacit knowledge, which often is embedded in the daily use of products and the development of design. This embeddedness presents researchers with few strategies for locating tacit knowledge. When asked how they prefer to use a product—say a backup camera—a user may articulate their desires in one way: "I want to be able to see all 360 degrees so that I don't have to use my rearview mirror." However, their tacit knowledge about how to parallel park may defy that explicit knowledge: When using the backup camera, the full 360-degree view proves distracting (and expensive), as the user moves between the rearview mirrors and the backup camera to effectively park or pull out. The driver may know that it's more practical to simply use the camera, but when they put their knowledge to work, they engage differently with the various technologies. For designers, then, exposing tacit knowledge requires putting the user in contexts of use, asking them to engage directly with the technologies so as to reveal their tacit knowledge and bring it to the surface.

Design Application

Tacit knowledge becomes important in multiple contexts: education, design, communication, and organizations, all of which seek the development of knowledge and attempt to assess or measure it. An industrial organization may want to understand why new members working on the floor aren't able to keep up as quickly with the production lines as others, only to find there is some unspoken, tacit knowledge about how to rotate through the line that veteran workers have

DOI: https://doi.org/10.37514/TPC-B.2022.1725.2.26

adopted through trial and error or through watching others. Paying attention to tacit knowledge may prompt managers to integrate alternative training that focuses on *know-how* rather than *know-that*, and in doing so, begin to onboard new employees more effectively and efficiently. Technical communicators developing instructional onboarding documentation or training materials might also find themselves engaging with tacit knowledge as they design or redesign materials.

■ Pedagogical Integration

Tacit knowledge exists in the nooks and crannies of daily work, defying the sometimes-obsessive value of metrics and big data. Understanding the role of tacit knowledge often requires focused qualitative data collection, either in *participatory design* observation sessions or ethnographic research studies. In educational spaces, active and experiential learning seek to engage students with the development of know-how, but few studies of how effectively tacit knowledge is imparted in the classroom exist. More is known about how tacit knowledge emerges in organizations, though certainly more research can challenge our often-limited view of knowledge.

Within technical and scientific communication pedagogy, tacit knowledge has been observed in terms of the rhetorical notion of phronesis. This Aristotelian idea of practical rationality in professional practice can emerge from a combination of theory (episteme), craft knowledge (techne), and situational experience. A productive way to simulate this combination of virtues in the pedagogical setting is by assigning students problem-based learning projects where they apply their developing expertise (craft and theory) and contextual wisdom (tacit knowledge) in order to address the case in point. Since tacit knowledge is strengthened by social interaction, individual intuition, and relationships, students should be encouraged to pay attention not just to the cognitive application in their problem-solving but also the affective dimension. To study how tacit knowledge affects students' learning, instructors may conduct qualitative research through student interviews or ethnography as a means to inform future course design.

■ References and Recommended Readings

Ambrosini, V. & Bowman, C. (2001). Tacit knowledge: Some suggestions for operationalization. *Journal of Management Studies, 38*(6), 811–829.

Cavusgil, S. T., Calantone, R. J. & Zhao, Y. (2003). Tacit knowledge transfer and firm innovation capability. *Journal of Business & Industrial Marketing, 18*(1), 6–21.

Durá, L., Perez, L. & Chaparro, M. (2019). Positive deviance as design thinking: Challenging notions of stasis in technical and professional communication. *Journal of Business and Technical Communication, 33*(4), 376–399.

Howells, J. (1996) Tacit knowledge. *Technology Analysis & Strategic Management, 8*(2), 91–106. https://doi.org/10.1080/09537329608524237.

Kimbell, L. (2012). Rethinking design thinking: Part II. *Design and Culture, 4*(2), 129–148.

Lam, A. (2000). Tacit knowledge, organizational learning and societal institutions: An integrated framework. *Organization Studies, 21*(3), 487–513.

Mareis, C. (2012). The epistemology of the unspoken: On the concept of tacit knowledge in contemporary design research. *Design Issues, 28*(2), 61–71.

Moore, K. R. & Elliott, T. (2016). From participatory design to a listening infrastructure: A case of urban planning and participation. *Journal of Business and Technical Communication, 30*(1), 58–84.

Smith, E. A. (2001). The role of tacit and explicit knowledge in the workplace. *Journal of Knowledge Management, 5*(4), 311–321.

Spinuzzi, C. (2002). Toward integrating our research scope: A sociocultural field methodology. *Journal of Business and Technical Communication, 16*(1), 3–32.

Spinuzzi, C. (2005). The methodology of participatory design. *Technical Communication, 52*(2), 163–174.

Tsoukas, H. (2005). Do we really understand tacit knowledge? In S. Little & T. Ray (Eds.), *Managing knowledge: An essential reader* (pp. 1–18). SAGE Publications.

27. Usability

Emma J. Rose
UNIVERSITY OF WASHINGTON TACOMA

Definition and Background

Usability describes the quality of a system—whether it is information, communication, a product, or a service—and how easy that system is to use. Usability means that a system meets the expectations of users and it has value that users can see for themselves (Dumas & Redish, 1999). Designing for usability requires three key principles: an early focus on users and tasks, empirical measurement, and iterative design (Gould & Lewis, 1985). Usability can be further broken down into several components that can be empirically measured. According to ISO 9241 (ISO, 2010), usability is made of three components: effectiveness, efficiency, and satisfaction. Whitney Quesenbery (2014) goes further, defining five dimensions of usability, referred to as the 5Es: effective, efficient, engaging, error tolerant, and easy to learn.

Usability as a concept has changed and evolved over time. Initially, usability, or usability engineering, was used to describe both the process of designing usability into a system and its evaluation (Nielsen, 1993). As the field has matured and the importance of involving people throughout the design process has become more visible, there has been a shift from talking about usability to user experience (Hartson & Pyla, 2012). Usability has been critiqued for being too narrowly defined (Sullivan, 1989) and being overly concerned with effectiveness and efficiency in a way that overlooks both nuance and cultural context (Dilger, 2006). User experience takes into account the full experience a person has with a product or service and the organization responsible for it. This broader view of the field that shifts from usability to user experience includes all the qualities that inform and influence that relationship between a person and their experience, which includes emotional, social, and cultural factors (Kuniavsky, 2007). Strong usability fosters connection between users and the product or service they are using, which can enhance their perception of the value associated with a product or organization (Acharya, 2017). For a deeper discussion on usability testing, see Bradley Dilger's entry on *testing* in this collection. For more on the process of designing for usability, see Jason Tham's chapter on *user-centered design*.

Design Application

The primary way to measure usability is through the applied research method of usability studies, also known as usability testing. A usability study can be

DOI: https://doi.org/10.37514/TPC-B.2022.1725.2.27

conducted on information, a product, a system, or a service, to evaluate its usability at any point during the design process. Typically, usability studies are either summative or formative (Barnum, 2010). In a summative usability study, the aim is to understand how a functional and completed system performs for the purpose of benchmarking and comparison. Formative usability studies are conducted when a system is under development and the goal is to make iterative improvements based on user feedback prior to its completion. During a typical usability study, participants are asked to attempt to perform tasks with the system while thinking out loud (Boren & Ramey, 2000). Researchers collect performance data such as time on task and task completion, in addition to verbal protocols and participants' ranking and ratings of the system. Beyond usability studies, there are additional research methods that can gather data to help design, evaluate, and improve the usability of a system, such as heuristic reviews, surveys, and analytics, just to name a few.

While usability was once primarily the purview of software and documentation, it has broadened to a variety of other contexts with their own unique considerations. Where usability does not solely mean ease of use, but also usefulness, which is imperative for design contexts that grapple with complexity (Mirel, 2004). Take civic online spaces, where the focus is to enhance citizen action. In these contexts, usability must take into account and support people's ability to take multiple perspectives, encourage users to engage in productive inquiry, and support complex decision making (Simmons & Zoetewey, 2012). Further, working in community-based organizations demonstrates the need to expand and tailor usability considerations so they are appropriate for the audience and context. In the case of working with multilingual immigrant audiences in the US who were signing up for health insurance, usability considerations shift to prioritize comprehension and an in-depth understanding of lived experience and sources of anxiety, rather than standard metrics like time on task or performance (Rose et al., 2017). Other scholars have concluded that complex contexts call for new usability methods and approaches. Healthcare settings call for usability methods that take into account the situated context that patients experience as well as a clear focus on quality of life (Melonçon, 2017). Beyond nuance in different domains, speculative usability calls attention to the relationships beyond individual human actors to include the relationships between objects and examine nonhuman agency to consider how they impact use and usability (Rivers & Söderlund, 2016).

■ Pedagogical Integration

In reviewing technical communication core teaching resources, Felicia Chong (2016) noted a "lack of productive discussion that focuses specifically on usability practices and instruction in the classroom" (p. 23). Although national surveys have shown that technical communication programs are increasingly requiring usability as a core or vital part of the modern curriculum, Chong argued that we—academics and industry practitioners—should collaborate to devise a shared plan for the future of usability pedagogy. Teaching about usability can include how to design for usability, through user-centered design or user experience, and how to evaluate usability through usability testing. A common approach to teaching usability testing is through client-based projects that can help students learn about the method while also highlighting the nuanced, rhetorical nature of usability work (Scott, 2008; Rose & Tenenberg, 2017). Students are typically assigned to work in teams to conduct a mini usability study (three to five test participants) on a client's product. This exercise exposes students to the process of testing the usability of a design, from identifying core usability problems to creating a test plan, running the test, and presenting findings and recommendations for improvement. For those who do not have the resources in terms of time and tools to conduct usability studies, students may perform heuristic (expert) evaluations and other "discount" usability methods (Nielsen, 1997).

■ References and Recommended Readings

Acharya, K. R. (2017). User value and usability in technical communication: A value-proposition design model. *Communication Design Quarterly Review, 4*(3), 26–34.

Barnum, C. (2010). *Usability testing essentials.* Morgan Kauffman.

Boren, M. T. & Ramey, J. (2000). Thinking aloud: Reconciling theory and practice. *IEEE Transactions on Professional Communication, 43*(3), 261–278.

Chong, F. (2016). The pedagogy of usability: An analysis of technical communication textbooks, anthologies, and course syllabi and descriptions. *Technical Communication Quarterly, 25*(1), 12–28.

Dilger, B. (2006). Extreme usability and technical communication. In J. B. Scott, B. Longo & K. Wills (Eds.), *Critical power tools: Technical communication and cultural studies* (pp. 47–69). SUNY Press.

Dumas, J. S. & Redish, J. C. (1999). *A practical guide to usability testing.* Intellect Books.

Gould, J. D. & Lewis, C. (1985, March). Designing for usability: Key principles and what designers think. *Communications of the ACM, 28*(3), 300–311.

Hartson, R. & Pyla, P. S. (2012). *The UX book: Process and guidelines for ensuring a quality user experience.* Elsevier.

ISO. (2010). ISO 9241–210:2010. Ergonomics of human–system interaction—Part 210: Human-centered design for interactive systems. https://www.iso.org/standard/52075.html.

Kuniavsky, M. (2007). User experience and HCI. In A. Sears & J. A. Jacko (Eds.), *The human–computer interaction handbook fundamentals: Evolving technologies, and emerging applications* (2nd ed., pp. 3–22). Lawrence Erlbaum.

Melonçon, L. K. (2017). Patient experience design: Expanding usability methodologies for healthcare. *Communication Design Quarterly Review, 5*(2), 19–28.

Mirel, B. (2004). *Interaction design for complex problem solving: Developing useful and usable software.* Morgan Kaufmann.

Nielsen, J. (1993). *Usability engineering.* Morgan Kaufmann.

Nielsen, J. (1997). *Discount usability for the web*. Nielsen Norman Group. https://www.nngroup.com/articles/web-discount-usability/.

Quesenbery, W. (2014). The five dimensions of usability. In M. Elbers (Ed.), *Content and complexity: Information design in technical communication* (pp. 81–102). Routledge.

Rivers, N. & Söderlund, L. (2016). Speculative usability. *Journal of Technical Writing and Communication, 46*(1), 125–146.

Rose, E. J., Racadio, R., Wong, K., Nguyen, S., Kim, J. & Zahler, A. (2017). Community-based user experience: Evaluating the usability of health insurance information with immigrant patients. *IEEE Transactions on Professional Communication, 60*(2), 214–231.

Rose, E. & Tenenberg, J. (2017). Making practice-level struggles visible: Researching UX practice to inform pedagogy. *Communication Design Quarterly, 5*(1), 89–97.

Scott, J. B. (2008). The practice of usability: Teaching user engagement through service-learning. *Technical Communication Quarterly, 17*(4), 381–412.

Simmons, W. M. & Zoetewey, M. W. (2012). Productive usability: Fostering civic engagement and creating more useful online spaces for public deliberation. *Technical Communication Quarterly, 21*(3), 251–276.

Sullivan, P. (1989). Beyond a narrow conception of usability testing. *IEEE Transactions on Professional Communication, 32*(4), 256–264.

28. User-Centered Design

Jason Tham
Texas Tech University

Definition and Background

User-centered design, or UCD, is born of the need to make user-facing products usable *and* desirable. The Interactive Design Foundation (n.d.) puts it this way:

> User-centered design (UCD) is an iterative design process in which designers focus on the users and their needs in each phase of the design process. In UCD, design teams involve users throughout the design process via a variety of research and design techniques, to create highly usable and accessible products for them. (n.p.)

Although UCD is almost always tethered to **usability** research, it is most concerned with architecting and engineering user experience (UX). UCD moves beyond usability testing or validation into engagement with user emotions, experience, and expectations. Within technical and professional communication (TPC) scholarship, UCD has garnered spotlights since the rise of personal computing in the early 1980s. UCD experts like Don Norman and Stephen Draper (1986) had led the UCD movement by asking researchers and designers to shift their focus from function and form to "thoughtful design of links between people, systems, and society" (Pea, 1987, p. 130). Robert Johnson (1998) urged technical communicators to pay attention to the complexity of user interactions even in the most mundane situation because they can reveal "the phenomena of technological use from [the user's] perspective" (p. 4). Today, TPC researchers study **contextual** as well as **participatory design** methods to better understand user requirements and then translate them into design guidelines (cf. Andrews et al., 2012; Rose, 2016; Walton, 2016).

There have been discussions and debates regarding the use of the word *user* vs. *human* such as in human-centered design (HCD). Citing Rob Kling and Susan Leigh Star (1998) and William B. Rouse (2007), Mark Zachry and Jan H. Spyridakis (2016) note that HCD focuses on the social dimension of user interaction with systems that UCD has sometimes overlooked. Simon Baron-Cohen (2011) criticizes that by making the human element invisible, UCD dehumanizes the user in interactive system experiences. Marina Yalanska (2018) of FAQ Design Platform (tubikstudio.com) takes on the slight nuances in the two terms and observes that "human-centered design is the process of things deeply based on general natural characteristics and peculiarities of human psychology and perception," while "user-centered design is [a] more

DOI: https://doi.org/10.37514/TPC-B.2022.1725.2.28

focused and concise version of human-centered design with deeper analysis of target audience" (n.p.). Yalanska summarizes that HCD and UCD work hand-in-hand; the idea is to first design for humans, then define the needs of the specific category of users. Nevertheless, the shared missions of UCD and HCD have left the semantic battle unresolved. Today, UCD remains a dominant term within the UX profession.

■ Design Application

The core idea of UCD is to involve the user(s) of a product early and throughout the design process. That way, the design team is always engaged in discussions about usability of the product from the perspective of the user. Arguably, the most important part of UCD is constantly asking "*Who* are we designing this product for?" and "How can we *help them* achieve a desirable experience with the product?" ISO 9241–210:2019 (Ergonomics of human-system interaction—Part 210: Human-centered design for interactive systems; see International Organization for Standardization, 2019) is the basis for UCD practices (Usability.gov, n.d.). Managed by the Digital Communication Division in the U.S. Department of Health and Human Services, Usability.gov (n.d.) provides recommendations for UX best practices, including the following general phases for UCD methodologies:

- Specify the context of use: Identify the people who will use the product, what they will use it for, and under what conditions they will use it.
- Specify requirements: Identify any business requirements or user goals that must be met for the product to be successful.
- Create design solutions: This part of the process may be done in stages, building from a rough concept to a complete design.
- Evaluate designs: Evaluation—ideally through usability testing with actual users—is as integral as quality testing is to good software development. (n.p.)

While there are no specifically assigned methods for each phase in UCD, any direct engagement with users and participatory methods— e.g., focus groups, **contextual inquiry**, and empathy mapping—are beneficial to the design process. According to the Interactive Design Foundation (n.d.), a mixture of investigative methods and tools (such as observations, surveys, and interviews) and generative ones (like brain/bodystorming) can help designers develop an understanding of user needs.

Further, a good user experience is a holistic user experience. The aim of UCD should be to capture and address a comprehensive user experience. Thus, the makeup of the design team should reflect diversity in professional expertise (e.g., psychologists, engineers, ethnographers, data analysts) as well as domain leaders like marketers, stakeholders, and of course, the users.

■ Pedagogical Integration

UCD is central to technical communication pedagogy as the field has been historically rooted in audience awareness and rhetorical appeals. To teach UCD principles and practices, instructors could model after Ann Shivers-McNair et al.'s (2018) approach, where students are assigned a collaborative design project to practice applying UCD principles. Similar to many recommendations made in other entries in this collection, students can be motivated to understand and empathize with users through problem-based design projects. To invoke UCD values, students need meaningful interaction with actual users who are affected by the contexts surrounding the design problem. Activities such as contextual inquiry, journey mapping, and *participatory design* can provide a basis for UCD in technical communication pedagogy. However, as Shivers-McNair et al. (2018) suggested, students should not only focus on UCD as course concepts but also reflect upon their own experiences in learning UCD, and how design practices in and outside the classroom can be held accountable.

Indeed, instructors also have to take into consideration that experiential learning with *actual users* for the purpose of UCD is a very difficult (if not impossible) task to do at many locations. Beyond the classroom, TPC students can learn UCD concepts via mentorship programs such as what Lee-Ann Kastman Breuch et al. (2022) called a "joint enterprise," where students are paired with industry UX professionals to collaborate on workplace projects. This sort of initiative can be beneficial for TPC programs, especially those that need real-world stakeholders to give students an authentic UCD experience.

■ References and Recommended Readings

Andrews, C., Burleson, D., Dunks, K., Elmore, K., Lambert, C. S., Oppegaard, B., Pohland, L., Saad, E. E., Scharer, J. S., Wery, R. L., Wesley, M. & Zobel, G. (2012). A new method in user-centered design: Collaborative prototype design process. *Journal of Technical Writing and Communication*, *42*(2), 123–142. http://dx.doi.org/10.2190 /TW.42.2.c.

Baron-Cohen, S. (2011). *Zero degrees of empathy*. Penguin Group.

Benyon, D. (2014). *Designing interactive systems: A comprehensive guide to HCI, UX, and interaction design* (3rd ed.). Pearson Education Limited.

Breuch, L. A. K., Duin, A. H. & Gresbrink, E. (2022). Real-world user experience: Engaging students and industry professionals through a mentor program. In K. Crane & K. C. Cook (Eds.), *User experience as innovative academic practice* (pp. 219–250). The WAC Clearinghouse; University Press of Colorado. https://doi.org/10.37514/TPC-B .2022.1367.2.10.

Interaction Design Foundation. (n.d.). User Centered Design. https://www.interaction -design.org/literature/topics/user-centered-design.

International Organization for Standardization. (2019). *ISO 9241–210:2019 (Ergonomics of human-system interaction—Part 210: Human-centered design for interactive systems)*. https://www.iso.org/standard/77520.html.

Johnson, R. R. (1998). *User-centered technology: A rhetorical theory for computers and other mundane objects*. SUNY Press.

Kling, R. & Star, S. L. (1998). Human centered systems in the perspective of organizational and social informatics. *Computers and Society, 28*(1), 22–29.

Norman, D. & Draper, S. W. (Eds.). (1986). *User centered system design: New perspectives on human-computer interaction*. Lawrence Erlbaum Associates.

Pea, R. D. (1987). Review of User centered system design: New perspectives on human-computer interaction, by D. A. Norman and S. W. Draper. *Journal of Educational Computing Research, 3*(1), 129–134.

Rose, E. (2016). Design as advocacy: Using a human-centered approach to investigate the need of vulnerable populations. *Journal of Technical Writing and Communication, 46*(4), 427–445.

Rouse, W. B. (2007). *People and organizations: Explorations of human-centered design*. John Wiley & Sons.

Shivers-McNair, A., Phillips, J., Campbell, A., Mai, H. H., Macy, J. F., Wenlock, J., Fry, S. & Guan, Y. (2018). User-centered design in and beyond the classroom: Toward an accountable practice. *Computers and Composition, 49*, 36–47. https://doi.org/10.1016/j.compcom.2018.05.003.

Usability.gov. (n.d.). *User-centered design basics*. https://www.usability.gov/what-and-why/user-centered-design.html.

UXMastery.com. (n.d.). *UX techniques*. https://uxmastery.com/resources/techniques/.

Walton, R. E. (2016). Supporting human dignity and human rights: A call to adopt the first principle of human-centered design. *Journal of Technical Writing and Communication, 46*(4), 402–426.

Yalanska, M. (2018). *Human-centered vs user-centered. Are the terms different?* FAQ Design Platform. https://tubikstudio.com/faq-design-platform-human-centered-vs-user-centered-are-the-terms-different/.

Zachry, M. & Spyridakis, J. H. (2016). Human-centered design and the field of technical communication. *Journal of Technical Writing and Communication, 46*(4), 392–401.

29. Wicked Problems

Lauren Garskie
GANNON UNIVERSITY

▌ Definition and Background

A key component of design thinking is the kinds of problems for which it is particularly suited. The problems design thinking attempts to address are referred to as wicked problems. Wicked problems are "wicked" in both the problems themselves and their solutions. Wicked problems are complex, ambiguous problems involving many stakeholders. They neither have easily identifiable, one-time solutions nor can they be solved simply with more information. Horst Rittel, a mathematician, designer, and teacher, is credited with defining "wicked problems" in the 1960s (Buchanan, 1992; Marback, 2009) and along with Melvin Webber suggested ten distinguishing properties of wicked problems (Rittel & Webber, 1973). Expanding on the understanding of what wicked problems are, Rittel explains they are ill-formulated, the information is confusing, there are many clients and decision makers with conflicting values, and ramifications in the whole system are confusing (as cited in Buchanan, 1992, p. 15). Richard Buchanan further underscores the indeterminacy of wicked problems. In reviewing Buchanan's work, Richard Marback (2009) brings attention to Buchanan's connection of design and rhetoric, arguing for rhetoric as a wicked problem: "Rhetoric is the study of the most wicked of all problems: making responsible use of the persuasive power inherent in all artifacts" (p. 402).

It is not just the problem itself that is wicked, however, as the solution is also part of what constitutes a wicked problem. Marback (2009) argues these problems as wicked "because they are never finally solvable" (p. 399); rather, they require resolution "over and over again" (Rittel & Webber, 1973, p. 160). These problems feature no clear, permanent solution, being what Carrie Leverenz (2014) calls irresolvably complex. Jim Purdy explains they "require recursive attention and consideration of contextual factors" (as cited in Pope-Ruark, 2019, p. 439). This recursivity is a result of "[adjusting] to changing social, cultural, technological, and human needs" (Cooke et al., 2020, p. 328). Instead of calling them "wicked," Stanford's d.school (2019) refers to these problems as "unbounded problems," summarizing them as complex, ambiguous, and messy. While differences exist between calling design problems wicked versus unbounded, the d.school emphasizes that the solutions for unbounded problems are both uncertain and unclear.

A core ability for the d.school (2019) is to navigate the ambiguity and "develop tactics to overcome ambiguity when needed." One such tactic Katherine McKiernan and Andra Steinbergs (2016) identified was "trust among stakeholders and

DOI: https://doi.org/10.37514/TPC-B.2022.1725.2.29

collaboration toward a shared goal as important characteristics for taming wicked problems" (p. 104). When working on what they identified as a "wicked environmental problem," Stuart Blythe et al. (2008) noted, "The situation demanded that all parties communicate honestly and effectively with one another" (p. 273). Additionally, the continual refining and adapting rather than focusing on a fixed end-point is part of the "design thinking mindset needed to find *sufficient* solutions" (Cooke et al., 2020, p. 328). For example, "a civic entrepreneur's proposed solution (in the form of a venture) cannot be entirely set in stone because the parameters of the wicked problem are always shifting and being redefined over time" (Gerding & Vealy, 2017, p. 303).

▪ Design Application

Nigel Cross (2011) highlights this relationship between problem and solution as a theme of design thinking and how designers think and work. Cross (2011) explains, "In order to formulate a design problem to be solved, the designer must frame a problematic design situation: set its boundaries, select particular things and relations for attention, and impose on the situation a coherence that guides subsequent moves" (p. 120). Charles Wickman (2014) also stresses the role of the individual "in deciding—or, in some cases, prescribing—how problems should be defined and how, therefore, they ought to be addressed" (p. 27). Designers must carefully set the **problem definition**, recognizing as a wicked problem though **iteration** is inherent as "a linear path from problem to solution does not exist in wicked problems" (Rose, 2016, p. 432). It is up to them to impose some sort of structure to these problems, which explains why the **testing** phase of design thinking is especially iterative. At the same time, the designer is having to consider perhaps competing interests. The ambiguity of the problem is "created by multiple, potentially competing interests designers and their clients . . . bring to the design task of creating a specific artifact" (Marback, 2009, p. 399). The designers are constructing the frame in this ambiguous situation, and it may be wrong.

In imposing some sort of structure to these problems, important to remember is, as Cross (2011) notes, how the solution is not always straightforward; instead, emergent properties are perceived in earlier solutions that were not consciously intended. Referring again to the indeterminacy of wicked problems, Buchanan (1992) emphasizes the "problem for designers is to conceive and plan what does not yet exist, and this occurs in the context of the indeterminacy of *wicked problems*, before the final result is known" (p. 19). Overall, the focus on problem-solving and the nature of the problem is key to design thinking.

Wickman (2014) notes global climate change, educational reform, and widespread unemployment all as examples of wicked problems. Specifically, Wickman provided the environmental catastrophe of the 2010 Gulf of Mexico oil spill as a wicked problem because it was "so complex in [its] causes and effects, [it] cannot necessarily be 'solved' in any simple sense of the term" (p. 24). Wickman found

Rittel and Webber's ten characteristics as a useful way for understanding the complexity of that problem. Applying those characteristics to these global concerns, or even more local community concerns, can be a way of showing "that making change in the world often requires us to move beyond a linear, problem/solution model of engagement" (Wickman, 2014, p. 39).

▋ Pedagogical Integration

Carrie Leverenz (2014) has demonstrated the available connections between pedagogy and wicked problems in terms of design thinking. Instructors may "design wicked assignments" that are "growing out of some external exigency" (Leverenz, 2014, pp. 6–7). The key to enacting meaningful learning via wicked problems is to adhere to the culture that supports design thinking, namely the courage to experiment with unknowns or ambiguity, and willingness to embrace *failing*. For students, this means taking up more complex design issues, tinkering with new tools or technologies, trying unattempted approaches, and venturing into new terrains—or, as the cliché goes, stepping out of their comfort zone. Instructors may support such efforts by providing scaffolding activities such as problem definition exercises, sprint ideation and design sessions, and *rapid prototyping* activities.

Stepping out of the comfort zone can mean taking on the more complex problems society faces. April Greenwood et al. (2019) argue, "Wicked problems are those that transcend any one discipline, institution, or community: for instance, poverty, generational homelessness, obesity, pollution" (p. 401). The technical communication classroom provides an ideal space for engaging with wicked problems (Wickman, 2014). Jason Tham (2021) notes how "many TPC [technical and professional communication] scholar-instructors are already practicing design-centric, problem-based pedagogy" (p. 393). In taking on such problems, Laquana Cooke et al. (2020) further emphasize the need for *iteration* as "problem solving in TPC is most effective when approached as an iterative process that meaningfully engages with stakeholders, teammates, and users" (p. 328). One will need "to continually adapt to user needs, unfamiliar tools, and material constraints to tackle the complexity of an ill-defined problem" (Cooke et al., 2020, p. 328). It is design thinking's iterative approach which makes it particularly well suited for wicked problems.

Additionally, Joseph Williams et al. (2013) argue for the importance of distinct and specific "authentic" audiences within the technical communication classroom. "Truly authentic audiences, however, are increasingly mixed, composed of constituents who have disparate interests and needs that must be addressed with multiple sophisticated appeals, arguments, and modalities" (Williams et al., 2013, p. 248). As emphasized, wicked problems involve multiple, often conflicting stakeholders. For example, Stuart Blythe et al. (2008) identified themselves as third-party expert reviewers who "tried to support various stakeholders' efforts to define, understand, and articulate their responses" (p. 273). The U.S. Army Corp of Engineers, the Technical Outreach Services for Communities, and the local community were all part of their wicked environmental problem. Design thinking's first principle of *empathy* and tools such as empathy mapping can provide ways for understanding users. Yingying Tang (2020) explains how "design thinking values users, not as merely passive consumers . . . but as co-creators whose voices, experiences, and needs can shape the design and use of technologies." Such consideration of the user also requires awareness of the lack of clear, permanent solutions for wicked problems. Jeffery Gerding and Kyle Vealey (2017) ask, "How do you persuade or motivate people to be financially and socially invested in a problem that, by definition, cannot be solved?" (p. 293). They examined how +POOL, "a recreational pool, filtration system, and floating laboratory," developed "hybrid solutions that may not necessarily resolve or provide closure to complex social problems but that instead continually adapt and evolve to keep pace with them" (p. 293).

The pedagogical goal for integrating wicked problems with the technical communication classroom is to spark *innovation* rather than stifle it. Thus, instructors should mind the gaps between student aspiration, the available means for creative tinkering, and the magnitude of the wicked problem undertaken. These components need to be balanced in order to foster a positive learning experience that leads to productive, innovative, and—even better—implementable outcomes.

■ References and Recommended Readings

Blythe, S., Grabill, J. T. & Riley, K. (2008). Action research and wicked environmental problems: Exploring appropriate roles for researchers in professional communication. *Journal of Business and Technical Communication, 22*(3), 272–298.

Buchanan, R. (1992). Wicked problems in design thinking. *Design Issue, 8*(2), 5–21. Original presented October 1990.

Cooke, L., Dusenberry, L. & Robinson, J. (2020). Gaming design thinking: Wicked problems, sufficient solutions, and the possibility space of games. *Technical Communication Quarterly, 29*(4), 327–340.

Cross, N. (2011). *Design thinking.* Berg.

d.school. (2019). *About.* https://dschool.stanford.edu/about/.

Gerding, J. M. & Vealey, K. P. (2017). When is a solution not a solution? Wicked problems, hybrid solutions, and the rhetoric of civic entrepreneurship. *Journal of Business and Technical Communication, 31*(3), 290–318.

Greenwood, A., Lauren, B., Knott, J. & DeVoss, D. N. (2019). Dissensus, resistance, and ideology: Design thinking as a rhetorical methodology. *Journal of Business and Technical Communication, 33*(4), 400–424.

Leverenz, C. S. (2014). Design thinking and the wicked problem of teaching writing. *Computers and Composition, 33*, 1–12.

Marback, R. (2009). Embracing wicked problems: The turn to design in composition studies. *College Composition and Communication, 61*(2), 397–419.

McKiernan, K. R. & Steinbergs, A. (2016). Scientists as audience: Science communicators as mediators of wicked problems. In J. Goodwin (Ed.), *Confronting the challenges of public participation: Issues in environmental, planning and health decision-making* (pp. 103–108). CreateSpace.

Overmyer, T. & Brock Carlson, E. (2019). Literature review: Design thinking and place. *Journal of Business and Technical Communication, 33*(4), 431–436.

Pope-Ruark, R. (2019). Design thinking in technical and professional communication: Four perspectives. *Journal of Business and Technical Communication, 33*(4), 437–455.

Rittel, H. W. J. & Webber, M. M. (1973). Dilemmas in a general theory of planning. *Policy Sciences, 4*, 155–169.

Rose, E. J. (2016). Design as advocacy: Using a human-centered approach to investigate the needs of vulnerable populations. *Journal of Technical Writing and Communication, 46*(4), 427–445.

Tang, Y. (2020). Promoting user advocacy through design thinking in the age of automated writing. In *SIGDOC '20: Proceedings of the 38th ACM International Conference on Design of Communication*. https://doi.org/10.1145/3380851.3416784.

Tham, J. C. K. (2021). Engaging design thinking and making in technical and professional communication pedagogy. *Technical Communication Quarterly, 30*(4), 392–406. https://doi.org/10.1080/10572252.2020.1804619.

Wickman, C. (2014). Wicked problems in technical communication. *Journal of Technical Writing and Communication, 44*(1), 23–42.

Williams, J., Rice, R., Lauren, B., Morrison, S., Van Winkle, K. & Elliot, T. (2013). Problem-based universal design for learning in technical communication and rhetoric instruction. *Journal of Problem Based Learning in Higher Education, 1*(1), 247–261.

Contributors

Emily F. Brooks (Ph.D., University of Florida) specializes in book history, children's literature and culture, and digital humanities. She has written several library guides and taught Arduino courses for middle schoolers at Girls Tech Camp, high schoolers at Gator Computing Camp, and university students at the Marston Science Library. She regularly incorporates teaching physical computing and digital fabrication in her courses.

Shannon Butts (Ph.D., University of Florida) is an Instructor at the University of Florida and a Senior Learning Designer with Elsevier. Her research and teaching examine how emerging technologies, such as augmented reality and 3D printing, create new literacy practices and opportunities for civic engagement. Shannon has published on critical making, decolonial data methods, remix writing, girls technology camps, and location-based writing.

Mary E. Caulfield (A.L.M., Harvard University) is a Lecturer in MIT's Writing, Rhetoric, and Professional Communications department. She works with university-level students on project-based classes in design and engineering and teaches critical thinking and research skills to advanced secondary-school students. She has spoken at conferences on writing, speaking, and teamwork and has moderated panels on project-based learning, youth, and the media. Prior to joining MIT, she was a writer in the consulting and software industries.

Devon Cook (Ph.D., Purdue University) is Assistant Professor of English at Penn State New Kensington. His research interests include writing technology, empirical methodology, new materialism, and design thinking. He teaches courses in writing, technical communication, and multimedia design. He is currently working on a cross-disciplinary collaboration that brings technical communication concepts into coding pedagogy for engineering and Information Sciences and Technology (IST) students.

Bradley Dilger (Ph.D., University of Florida) is Professor of English at Purdue University. He is one of the co-founders of the Corpus & Repository of Writing (writecrow.org), a web-based archive for empirical research and professional development in writing studies. Crow researchers are also exploring methods for interdisciplinary collaboration in writing research. With Neil Baird, he studies writing transfer, focusing on writers' transitions from academic to professional environments.

Lauren Garskie (Ph.D., Bowling Green State University) is Assistant Professor of English and the Writing Intensive Coordinator at Gannon University. In addition to first-year and upper-level writing courses, she teaches as part of the minor in innovation and creativity, where team-taught courses engage students in the design thinking process and mindset. Her research interests include design literacies, digital rhetoric, collaboration, writing across the curriculum/ writing-enrichned curriculum (WAC/WEC), and writing pedagogy.

Thomas M. Geary (Ph.D., University of Maryland) is Professor of English at the Virginia Beach campus of Tidewater Community College, where he teaches composition, rhetoric, technical writing, developmental writing, and humanities courses. Tom serves as the editor of *Inquiry*, a peer-reviewed journal for faculty, staff, and administrators in Virginia's community colleges. He has published on soundwriting, electracy, online writing instruction, peer review, writing transfer, and compassionate pedagogy.

Krys Gollihue (Ph.D., North Carolina State University) is a technical marketer and content writer for Red Hat, Inc., a subsidiary group of IBM that provides open-source software solutions to enterprise businesses. They were formerly an Assistant Professor at University of North Alabama, and a Marion L. Brittain Postdoctoral Teaching Fellow at the Georgia Institute of Technology (Georgia Tech).

Andrew Kulak (Ph.D., Virginia Tech) is an Associate with the cybersecurity firm Triple Point Security and an adjunct professor in the Department of Computer Science at Virginia Tech. His research interests include technical communication, human-computer interaction, human-centered design, and rhetorics of technology. He has published and presented on video games, social media, online instructional design, information security, and digital research methods and ethics. He is co-editor of *The Pokémon Go Phenomenon: Essays on Public Play in Contested Spaces* from McFarland.

Ashanka Kumari (Ph.D., University of Louisville) is Director of Writing and Assistant Professor of English, Composition and Rhetoric at Texas A&M University–Commerce, where she mentors, researches, and teaches graduate and undergraduate students topics including composition theory, antiracist pedagogies, nonfiction, professional writing, and multimodal composing Her work has appeared in *WPA Journal*; *Kairos: A Journal of Rhetoric, Technology, and Pedagogy*; *Composition Studies*; and *Journal of Popular Culture*, among other journals and edited collections.

Jack T. Labriola (Ph.D., Texas Tech University) is a former Assistant Professor of Technical Communication and currently works as a Senior UX Researcher at Truist. He has previously presented and published on user experience, content strategy, and content management systems.

Liz Lane (Ph.D., Purdue University) is Assistant Professor and coordinator of Writing, Rhetoric, and Technical Communication at the University of Memphis. She teaches courses such as Document Design, Web Design, and Online Writing, and undergraduate and graduate seminars in technical writing. She co-founded and served as co-managing editor of *Spark: A 4C4Equality Journal*, an open-access venue of activist rhetorics in writing studies. She has published widely on activism, digital rhetoric, and technical communication.

Jason Luther (Ph.D., Syracuse University) is Assistant Professor of Writing Arts at Rowan University. His research focuses on writing technologies, history of media, DIY culture, self-publishing, publics, and sound writing.

Zarah C. Moeggenberg (Ph.D., Washington State University) is Assistant Professor of Technical Communications and Interaction Design at Metropolitan State University (Minnesota), where she teaches courses in content strategy, document design, editing, and medical writing. Her courses immerse students in considering positionality, privilege, and power—how these relate to issues of equity and justice within technical communication. Her current scholarship focuses on tracing rhetorics of the body and embodiment within technical communication, graduate student mentoring for the job market, digital literacies, and social justice-based pedagogy. Her scholarship is concerned with queer and feminist rhetorical practices in technical communication, particularly in medical writing.

Kristen R. Moore (Ph.D., Purdue University) is Associate Professor of Technical Communication in the Departments of Engineering Education and English at the University at Buffalo. Her research focuses on the public forms of technical communication, with a particular interest in how to increase the participation, efficacy, and justice of public technical communication. Her research has been published in a range of edited collections and many journals, including *Journal of Technical Writing and Communication*, *Technical Communication Quarterly*, and *IEEE Transactions on Professional Communication*. Most recently, she co-authored *Technical Communication After the Social Justice Turn: Building Coalitions for Action*.

Jeff Naftzinger (Ph.D., Florida State University) is Assistant Professor of Rhetoric, Composition & Writing at Sacred Heart University in Fairfield, Connecticut, where he teaches courses on digital writing and rhetoric, everyday writing, and first-year writing. He has published and presented on topics related to defining and illustrating everyday writing, sustaining multimodal composing, and writing in digital spaces.

April L. O'Brien (Ph.D., Clemson University) is Assistant Professor of Technical Communication at Sam Houston State University. Her research spans a variety of social justice-related concerns, including intersections within public memory, space/place, community writing, and technical communication. Her portfolio can be viewed at aprilobrien.net, and she tweets @april_rhetor.

Cody Reimer (Ph.D., Purdue University) is Associate Professor of English at University of Wisconsin-Stout, where he teaches in the Professional Communication and Emerging Media undergraduate program and Technical and Professional Communication master's program. He serves on the editorial board for *Communication Design Quarterly*, the peer-reviewed research publication of the Association for Computing Machinery (ACM) Special Interest Group for Design of Communication (SIGDOC). His research explores the intersection of technical writing in videogames.

Emma J. Rose (Ph.D., University of Washington Seattle) is Associate Professor in Technical Communication and User Experience Design in the School of Interdisciplinary Arts & Sciences at the University of Washington Tacoma. Her research is motivated by a commitment to social justice and inclusive design. She focuses on broadening participation in user experience design through participatory and inclusive research methods.

Jennifer Sano-Franchini (Ph.D., Michigan State University) is Gaziano Family Legacy Professor of Rhetoric and Writing and Associate Professor of English at West Virginia University. Her scholarly interests are in interaction design, user experience, cultural rhetorics and/of technology, and Asian American rhetoric. She has published in journals including *Technical Communication, Enculturation, Rhetoric Review*, and *Rhetoric, Professional Communication, and Globalization*, as well as edited collections such as *Rhetoric and Experience Architecture* and *Rhetoric and the Digital Humanities*. Prior to going into academia, she spent seven years as the design consultant for a small copy company in Honolulu, Hawai'i.

Adam Strantz (Ph.D., Purdue University) is Assistant Professor of Interactive Media Studies and Professional Writing at Miami University in Oxford, OH. His major areas of interest include data visualization, graphic design, accessibility, maps, and mobile technologies. He is currently exploring the intersections of design thinking, LEGO, and serious play.

Rachael Sullivan (Ph.D., University of Wisconsin-Milwaukee) is Assistant Professor of Communication and Digital Media at Saint Joseph's University, where she teaches courses in digital ethics, visual rhetoric, and design. Her research addresses topics such as interface design history, rhetorics of software and code, internet culture, and feminist-materialist approaches to composition and design. Her work has appeared in *Present Tense* and *Computers & Composition*.

Jason Tham (Ph.D., University of Minnesota) teaches user experience design, usability research, and instructional design at Texas Tech University. He studies the uses and implications of design thinking approaches—including empathic inquiry, iterative development, and radical collaboration—in technical communication pedagogy and professional practice. He is author of *Design Thinking in Technical Communication* (Routledge; ATTW Series) and co-author of *Designing Technical and Professional Communication* (Routledge, with Deborah Andrews) and *Collaborative Writing Playbook* (Parlor Press, with Joe Moses).

Luke Thominet (Ph.D., Wayne State University) is Assistant Professor of Writing and Rhetoric in the English Department at Florida International University. His work examines user experience during video game development, applications of design thinking to pedagogy and academic program development, and plain language in patient-physician discourse. His research has appeared in *Technical Communication Quarterly, Journal of Technical and Business Communication, Communication Design Quarterly*, and in the edited collections *Effective Teaching of Technical Communication* and *User Experience as Innovative Academic Practice*.

Matthew A. Vetter (Ph.D., Ohio University) is Associate Professor of English at Indiana University of Pennsylvania, where he is affiliate faculty in the Composition and Applied Linguistics Ph.D. program. He has published numerous articles on one of the most widely known collaborative writing projects, Wikipedia. Vetter is a co-editor of the open-access composition textbook *Writing Spaces*.

Ian R. Weaver (Ph.D., Texas Tech University) is Assistant Professor of English at the University of North Carolina Wilmington, where he teaches science writing and communication in the professional writing program. Collaborating with applied scientists, his research considers how participatory design can help authorities communicate uncertainty, risk, and crisis more effectively. His research with National Weather Service (NWS) meteorologists and a volunteer social media support team has developed practical heuristics for scientists working with public users during severe weather.

Stephanie West-Puckett (Ph.D., East Carolina University) is Assistant Professor of Writing and Rhetoric at the University of Rhode Island. She teaches cultural rhetorics and directs the First-Year Writing (FYW) program, which is heavily influenced by her research and participation in makerspaces. She charts a professional course that tacks between failing forward and failing sideways and publishes on writing program administration; digital, queer, and maker-centered composition and assessment practices; and open-access learning through connectivist massive open online courses (MOOCs).

Scott Wible (Ph.D., Pennsylvania State University) is Associate Professor of English, Director of the Professional Writing Program, and Faculty Fellow in the Academy for Innovation and Entrepreneurship at the University of Maryland, College Park.

Emily Wierszewski (Ph.D., Kent State University) is Associate Professor of English and Composition and Director of the Undergraduate Writing Program at Seton Hill University in Greensburg, PA. She is passionate about transmedia, narrative, and rhetoric. She's currently working on a collection of digital stories about the value and purpose of "making." She teaches in the English and Digital Humanities programs at her institution.